D1562789

PRINCIPLES OF
INSTRUMENTAL LOGIC

PRINCIPLES OF INSTRUMENTAL LOGIC

John Dewey's Lectures in

Ethics and Political Ethics, 1895–1896

Edited by Donald F. Koch

Southern Illinois University Press

Carbondale and Edwardsville

Printed in the United States of America

01   00   99   98   4   3   2   1

Library of Congress Cataloging-in-Publication Data

Dewey, John, 1859–1952.
Principles of instrumental logic :
John Dewey's lectures in ethics and political ethics,
1895–1896 / edited by Donald F. Koch.
p.   cm.
Includes bibliographical references and index.
1. Ethics.   2. Political ethics.
I. Koch, Donald F., 1938– . II. Title.
BJ1571.D47   1998
170—DC21   97-48994
CIP
ISBN 0-8093-2173-4 (cloth : alk. paper)

The paper used in this publication meets the minimum requirements of
American National Standard for Information Sciences—Permanence
of Paper for Printed Library Materials, ANSI Z39.48-1984. ∞

Contents

Part Two.
Lectures on Political Ethics: Spring Quarter 1896

Preface

THE TWO SETS OF LECTURES that follow are taken from the collection of Dewey material at Morris Library, Southern Illinois University. According to the description in the *University of Chicago Annual Register, July, 1894–95, with Announcements for 1895–96*, the Logic of Ethics course was given in the 1895 Fall Quarter and the Political Ethics course in the 1896 Spring Quarter. Here are the course descriptions as given in the *Register*.

> 13. *The Logic of Ethics.*—This course will undertake a critical examination of the nature and conditions of a scientific treatment of ethics. It will involve a discussion of the relation of ethics to physical and social science, and of the methods appropriate to ethical inquiry and statement. The chief ethical categories will be analyzed, the following concepts being examined with reference to their content and scientific validity: Value, natural and moral; Standards of value and their application; the relation of Ideal to Fact in the ethical judgment; Law, physical and moral; Freedom, in its relation to law, causality, and responsibility. For graduate students.

> 15. *Political Ethics.*—This course will approach the problems of ethics from the standpoint of social organization, as the preceding one does from the standpoint of the individual agent. The two courses are thus complementary. It will deal (1) with ethical statics, or the organized moral order, including a discussion of the ethical significance of social institutions, and of rights and duties as related to institutions; and (2) with ethical dynamics, or the nature and conditions of moral progress in society as a whole. For graduate students.

In between these two courses, Dewey taught course 14, *The Psychology of Ethics*, which, according to the *Register*, "will give a review of the chief ethical problems and results so far as these can be stated in terms of individual psychology. It will include particularly the psychology of volition, taking up such topics as impulse, intention, deliberation, effort, desire and pleasure, motive, choice, and overt action." There are no extant notes for this course, perhaps because the extended description in the *Register* indicated that it would be for class reports and discussion.

   The lectures on the Logic of Ethics are from a forty-eight-page, typewritten, single-spaced, hectographed copy, originally part of the H. Heath Bawden Collection at St. Louis University. Although internal evidence suggests a careful transcription, the unknown transcriber made little or no effort to edit the material for proper punctuation within sentences, provide subheadings for the different topics discussed, or even divide the material into paragraphs. There is one long paragraph from page 8 to page 16.

   The lectures on Political Ethics are taken from a faint carbon copy of an eighty-three-page typescript available in the Morris Library Special Collections at Southern Illinois University at Carbondale. Internal evidence suggests a relatively careful transcriber, although, as indicated in editorial notes, occasional queries arise. Unlike the lectures on the Logic of Ethics, the material on Political Ethics was originally divided into paragraphs, albeit not always with due care.

   What was the original source of this material? The brevity of the material leads us to rule out the hypothesis that the lectures are a verbatim transcript of the entire course. The editors of Volume 5 of Dewey's *Early Works* suggest that the course in the Logic of Ethics is "apparently condensed."[1] If so, who condensed it? The material in both sets of lectures is very abstract and difficult, while at the same time clear. It seems unlikely that even a competent person familiar with Dewey's work could do such a good job. Moreover, it is likely that a person willing to do this job so well would have taken greater care to undertake ordinary editing chores.

   One possibility regarding the Logic of Ethics lectures (and perhaps the lectures on Political Ethics as well) is that Dewey was reading from or paraphrasing another of his works in the logic of inquiry. Perhaps he was reading to the class in order to provide subject matter for discussion. Volumes in J. H. Muirhead's "Library of Philosophy Series" that were published between 1892 and 1897 (and perhaps even later) give a "List of Works in Preparation" immediately before the title page, including *Principles of Instrumental Logic*, by John Dewey, Ph.D., Professor of Philosophy, University of Chicago. This volume was never published, and the title has been assigned to these lectures.

   There is another set of Dewey lectures on logic that serve as a possible candidate for the title *Principles of Instrumental Logic*. The 1899–1900 "Lectures on Logic" are an account of the theory of judgment as the key to inquiry in general, with only a few incidental references to ethical inquiry.[2] These lectures repeat the criticism of F. H. Bradley and Bernard Bosanquet contained in the logic lectures to follow, and they expand Dewey's theory of judgments. It is unfortunate that, at this time, Dewey's work in formal logical theory left out discussion of the role of ethical inquiry as an aspect of inquiry in general. So, for example, the 1903 volume, *Studies in Logical Theory*, was published separately from the important article, "Logical Conditions of a Scientific Treatment of Morality," published during the same year.[3]

Dewey's moral philosophy was a lifetime project. Taken overall, the result is complex, detailed, and very long. He seemed to assume that his readers were familiar with his previous publications as well as his unpublished lectures. With each successive publication, he does not identify what he has retained from previous publications, what he has rejected, or what is new. But in confronting this material, we must keep in mind that Dewey is attempting a wholesale reconstruction of traditional moral philosophy. The latter is reflected in the habitual assumptions of most contemporary inquirers: the distinction, made to the point of dualism, between moral inquiry and scientific inquiry; the belief that the essence of morality can be known in advance of the complex situations to which it is applied; and the effort to seek a justification or grounding for obligation, rights, or justice independently of situations that call for judgments about them.

It is virtually impossible for inquirers steeped in the tradition of western moral inquiry to avoid employing these assumptions. Now compare a contrasting set of habitual assumptions associated with Dewey's approach to moral inquiry: the recognition of the need to evaluate the process of moral inquiry itself; the acknowledgement of genuine, morally problematic situations, with the goal of an inquiry that responds to the problem; the search for instrumental categories (including the terms of moral language) to guide the inquiry; and the use of creative intelligence to reconstruct the problematic situation and deal with the difficulty. It is hard to see how these guiding assumptions will ever be accepted as habitual unless we carefully evaluate the reconstructed approach to inquiry in general, and moral inquiry in particular, that Dewey spent his life working out.

I would like to thank Larry Hickman, director of the Center for Dewey Studies at Southern Illinois University at Carbondale, for his encouragement and cooperation in furthering the publication of these lectures. They are reprinted with the permission of the Center for Dewey Studies, Southern Illinois University, Carbondale, Illinois. The Special Collections staff at Morris Library, Southern Illinois University at Carbondale, was very helpful in locating Dewey material. I would also like to thank Jordy Rocheleau for help in proofreading and Alexandria Weinbrecht for copyediting the manuscript.

Notes

1. *EW,* 5:cxxxi.

2. Steven A. Nofsinger has edited these lectures, along with a long analytical introduction, as a Ph.D. dissertation (Michigan State University, 1989).

3. For Dewey's *Studies in Logical Theory,* see *MW,* 2:293–375. "Logical Conditions of a Scientific Treatment of Morality" (*MW,* 3:3–39) is a sequel to another important article on the Logic of Ethics, "The Evolutionary Method as Applied to Morality" *(MW,* 2:1–38).

A Note on Editorial Methods

THE EDITORIAL DECISION to number each paragraph of the lectures is a device for separating and identifying material that appears as a thicket of words in the two original typescripts. It also provides an easily identifiable reference point for a particular sequence of passages. One problem concerns the addition of words such as 'the,' 'is,' and others where it appears the notetaker left them out for purposes of convenience. Silent additions of these terms were made where the meaning seems clear. Brackets are added to Dewey's text in cases where the situation calls for editorial judgment. Material in parentheses is by Dewey. Title headings without brackets are taken from the typescript, and others added by the editor are in brackets.

Abbreviations of Dewey's Published Works

EW   *The Early Works: 1882–1898.* 5 vols. Carbondale: Southern Illinois University Press, 1969–72.

LE   *Lectures on Ethics: 1900–1901.* Edited by Donald F. Koch. Carbondale: Southern Illinois University Press, 1991.

LPPE   *Lectures on Psychological and Political Ethics: 1898.* Edited by Donald F. Koch. New York: Hafner Press, 1976.

LW   *The Later Works: 1925–1952.* 17 vols. Carbondale: Southern Illinois University Press, 1981–90.

MW   *The Middle Works: 1899–1924.* 15 vols. Carbondale: Southern Illinois University Press, 1976–83.

Part One
Lectures on the Logic of Ethics
Fall Quarter 1895

Editor's Introduction to the
Lectures on the Logic of Ethics

An Overall Approach to Inquiry

THE PROGRAM for a philosophy of inquiry set forth in these lectures is a remarkable achievement in comprehensiveness, depth, and integration of subject matters often discussed separately and without regard for their place within the process of human experience at large. It provides the basis for a logic of experimental inquiry to be shared by scientific and moral inquirers alike. Further, it offers a positive program for doing away with the alleged dualism between moral and scientific inquiry, while maintaining the distinction between them. Its starting point is the unity of human experience as expressed in the ordinary judgment with a subject, copula, and predicate. This judgment is inherently valuational, a response to a problematic situation.[1] The subject, copula, and predicate mode of expression allows for variations in the function the judgment can serve, including scientific and intellectual, moral, and aesthetic judgments. There remains the religious phase of experience as the realization that any specific phase is an expression of the whole. In sum, inquiry starts with the unity shared by all judgments when taken as a response to the problematic and makes distinctions within this unity in order to further the inquiry.

The lectures are a *tour de force*. In their original form, they take forty-eight typewritten, single-spaced pages. In this brief space, Dewey works out a reconstruction of traditional ethical theory that rocks it to its very foundations and then goes on to develop an alternative approach to moral inquiry. The cryptic style of expression is initially off-putting, as if the author of these lectures had absorbed a mass of specific detail and then tried to summarize it in a series of concentrated, abstract statements. The reader expects a more detailed explanation that is not forthcoming. Yet, this cryptic style may be part of an effort to give brief expression to a comprehensive vision that would likely be lost to the reader if expressed at great length. Each statement is coherent, and the reader gets the sense that important issues are dealt with rather than postponed to some indefinite future. The reader familiar with Dewey's later works can return to them again and come to regard them as a working out of the singular, coherent, vision presented here.[2]

One problem for the contemporary reader of Dewey is to locate this vision as a starting point for further inquiry. He did not regard his work as the final words of an irrefutable authority, but as an invitation to additional inquiries into the reconstruction of philosophy[3] that would be instrumental for the "common man" who has to face and deal with the "problems of men." The term 'vision,' as I use it here, suggests an organized starting point that can serve as an instrument, or device to be used in organizing, for more specific inquiries. (We know that Dewey himself used this standpoint in his complex 1898 and 1901 "Lectures on the Psychology of Ethics" and his 1898 "Lectures on Political Ethics," given in the years immediately after the lectures that follow, as well as in his numerous articles and books.) These more specific inquiries in turn provide an approach to go about dealing with human problems. The philosopher's role is not to provide answers to these problems, but to develop instruments of inquiry that enable others to work out hypotheses and to reconstruct the problematic situations that mark the starting point of inquiry.

But it is not easy to get a grasp of Dewey's vision, and these lectures provide a helpful starting point. In the opening pages of his monumental treatise, *Logic: The Theory of Inquiry* (1938), he asserts that the "ultimate subject-matter" of logical theory is expressed by the words "*is, is-not, if-then, only (none but), and, or, some-all.*" In the concluding paragraph he asserts that "failure to institute a logic based ... upon the operations of inquiry has enormous cultural consequences." Failure to take up scientific methods of inquiry in particular results in "cultural waste, confusion, and distortion ... in all fields." Finally, "these considerations reinforce the claim of logical theory, as the theory of inquiry, to assume and hold a position of primary human importance." (The term 'human' can be construed to refer to the problems in individual and social life that are designated as moral.)

Meanwhile, in the body of the *Logic,* the discussion of subject, copula, and predicate that serves as the starting point for the 1895 "Lectures on the Logic of Ethics" is set forth in chapter 7.[4] Although the view worked out in the chapter can be regarded as a refinement of his 1895 position, Dewey makes no provision in it for the reader who is concerned about the "primary human importance" of logic and the "enormous cultural consequences," the "cultural waste, confusion, and distortion" involved in neglecting it. The implication is that the subject matter is exclusively technical and nonmoral in import. But, as we discover from reading these lectures, logic, as the general theory of inquiry, has an enormous moral significance, because it requires us to reconstruct our approach to inquiry in humane or moral subject matters.

The place of Dewey's logic of inquiry within his treatment of moral subject matters has not yet been emphasized.[5] These lectures on the Logic of Ethics help us to correct this omission, while at the same time they provide a clearer understanding of what he is trying to do.

Most moral theorists have followed the lead of Aristotle, Kant, Henry Sidgwick, and many others in starting with the moral judgments we already make. If these are not correct as such, they at least provide a kind of checkpoint for the evaluation of the moral ideals and standards that are alleged by theorists to be implicit in these judgments. The outcome of theoretical inquiry can then be utilized to give guidance in dealing with more difficult moral problems. These allegedly problematic situations can be resolved by the application of ideals and standards we already accept.

This approach is unsatisfactory in two ways. First, as it is characteristically employed, it does not allow for justification of the moral ideals and standards themselves, other than the justification implicit in the belief that they do, after all, express what we mean by morality. There is no difficulty so far, providing we presuppose that we are all united in our sense of what is moral. But when there is disagreement, either about the general meaning of morality or its application in specific situations, effort to resolve the disagreement is limited to trying to convince an opponent that his or her account of morality is not in accord with the account of morality he or she already implicitly assumes. But if, for whatever reason, we abandon the assumption of the unity of morality, we are forced to concede that moral inquiry is helpless in the face of moral disagreements that are expressions of disunity. There is no more inquiry to be done.

The second unsatisfactory aspect of this approach also stems from the tendency to start with moral beliefs. If we do so, examination of moral language, taken as such, suggests that moral subject matter is cut off from scientific inquiry. The alleged value of this conclusion for moral theorists is that it establishes morality as an autonomous field of inquiry. The unsatisfactory aspect is that the benefits of scientific inquiry are no longer open to the moral philosopher.

In these lectures, Dewey deals with these two difficulties by developing the theme that both moral and scientific judgments have in common the fact that they are judgments, each with a subject, copula, and predicate. He reconstructs the accounts of judgment in Lotze, Bradley, and Bosanquet, and in so doing Dewey makes a transition from logic as a theory of judgment that attempts to explain the relation of a fixed datum to a fixed universal (for example, the analysis of the judgment "This is an envelope") to logic as a theory of inquiry illustrating the function of judgment as a response to a problem. The copula that links subject and predicate is dynamic. It represents a division of labor in the effort to control experience. It does not, as in traditional Aristotelean logic, express a link between subject and predicate as separate and fixed subject matters. The need for control in dealing with the problematic is a shared link between scientific and moral inquiry. Moral inquiry in particular does not seek to discover and characterize a fixed moral subject matter. Instead of ending moral inquiry with the defense of a particular position as moral, and then having to contend with the problem that occurs when some people disagree and/or refuse to act morally, moral inquiry *starts* with the problematic and then develops the distinction between scientific and moral inquiry as instruments in locating the problem. So far as moral inquiry is a response to the problematic, it must supply a proposed solution. That is, moral inquiry also has a scientific aspect, because it is concerned about the formulation of successful hypotheses as a means to the solution of the problem.

At this point we should raise a cautionary warning. The program in these lectures is not repeated in Dewey's later works as such.[6] Shall we then conclude that the program is a kind of evolutionary failure, a variation that did not succeed? Or does it play a significant role in the development and overall coherence of Dewey's philosophical approach? The beginning of a case for the latter view is made by Dewey himself in his autobiographical essay, "From Absolutism to Experimentalism." He remarks about the "struggle between a native inclination towards the schematic and formally logical and those incidents of personal experience that compelled me to take account of actual material." He goes on to say that, although he had to struggle against that native bent, perhaps "the emphasis upon the concrete, empirical, and 'practical'" in his later writings is the outcome of that struggle. Yet, he also asserts that his "formal interest persisted" and that his concern is to "weld together" the formal and the practical or material. In sum, "there was an inner demand for an intellectual technique that would be consistent and yet capable of flexible adaptation to the concrete diversity of experienced things."[7] No doubt the lectures that follow emphasize the "schematic and formal" and the "intellectual technique" at the expense of inquiry into "concrete diversity."

But do they go too far in the direction of the formal? I think not. As we will see in the remarks to follow, Dewey's program to overcome the dualisms that frustrate effective inquiry require, as a formal condition of consistency, a unified starting point. Distinctions are made within a unity. The fundamental problem is to find an expression for the unity within the diversity of concrete experience. In other words, you have to allow for a universal aspect of experience, while allowing for specific problematic situations to arise within that unity.[8]

Historical Background

The development of Dewey's moral philosophy in the last decade of the nineteenth century and the first few years of the twentieth century constitutes one of the most remarkable efforts in the history of philosophical inquiry. He rejects the objective idealism of his early years and works out an initial version of instrumentalism that he calls experimental idealism. This endeavor required the development of a dynamic psychology of the individual-in-the-process-of-reconstruction to replace his earlier idealist psychology. No longer does individual "will" function to attain self-realization as the reproduction of the will of an absolute spirit that is already fully realized. The individual is now to be regarded as an initiating agent, responding to a problematic situation, using intelligence to overcome difficulty, and seeking a resolution of the problem faced. Moral ends are no longer given in advance, either in the form of a perfect absolute spirit to be emulated or in the form of unchanging moral principles. As we shall see in the "Lectures on Political Ethics" to follow, the social situation in which the individual functions as an organ for initiation may or may not provide an adequate stimulus to the success of these initiatives. At any rate, a system of rights and duties evolves within the social organism, so that the individual both benefits from the whole and has responsibilities within it.

The social side of human experience also has to be reworked. The idealist standpoint that society already is an organism, wherein each organ (either the individual or existing social institutions) both contributes to and benefits from the whole, is modified so that society has an organic character in which tension between the various organs provides a stimulus for intelligent reconstruction. The economic and educational processes are the chief agents of social reconstruction. Dewey's effort to improve the educational process through the experimental "Dewey School" at the University of Chicago, and his many publications on education during this period, are enduring contributions.

Our interest in the lectures to follow is in the development of Dewey's logical standpoint and his approach to inquiry. In *How We Think* (1910), he sets forth "five logically distinct steps" in the process of thinking:

  (i)   a felt difficulty;
  (ii)   its location and definition;
  (iii)   suggestion of possible solutions;

(iv) development by reasoning of the bearings of the suggestion;
(v) further observation and experiment leading to its acceptance or rejection; that is, the conclusion of belief or disbelief.[9]

We can use this schema to explore the difficulties to which Dewey was responding. His rejection of absolute idealism left him with a number of barriers to the development of an adequate moral theory. Each difficulty had to be located and a suggestion for its solution given. The test of the solution is experimental: Does the solution, when it is utilized, respond to and solve the problem?

What were these "felt" difficulties Dewey had to cope with? The question engages our interest, because each difficulty can be reformulated as a specific question that must be answered if instrumentalism is to be an adequate approach to moral inquiry. The questions were formulated and the answers given during the years 1892 through 1903. Dewey's later moral writings, beginning with the textbook _Ethics_ (1908),[10] avoided discussion of inquiry _qua_ inquiry. Hence the appearance of "gaps" in those later writings that suggest unanswered questions and unsolvable difficulties. Specifically, the two editions (1908, _MW_, vol. 5; 1932, _LW_, vol. 7) of the popular textbook _Ethics_, co-written by Dewey and James H. Tufts, avoided discussion of the theory of inquiry. Moreover, the theory presented was set forth as both a criticism and a reconstruction of the major theories in the history of ethics. Therefore, it is easy to get the impression that it is just one more theory that is presented, rather than a revolutionary approach to ethical inquiry that rejects previous methods.

The opening page of Dewey's 1892 article, "Green's Theory of the Moral Motive," describes a general difficulty for the ethical theorist. "Ethics" as the "theory of practice" appears to have only two approaches to inquiry, both of them unacceptable. The first approach is the attempt to set up a body of "rigid rules . . . with the object of having always some precept which will tell just what to do."[11] But "it is seen to be impossible that any body of rules should be sufficiently extensive to cover the whole range of action," and the result is a "casuistry . . . which is so demoralizing as to . . . destroy the grace and play of life by making conduct mechanical." The second approach reacts by abandoning effort to deal with "the guidance of action" and attempts instead "to analyze the general conditions under which morality is possible; to determine . . . the nature of that universe which permits or requires moral action."

This dilemma also occurs in contemporary discussion. Despite the substantial effort in recent years to develop a practical ethics to deal with contemporary moral and political problems, there are many people who ask whether moral philosophers have a special ability to give adequate answers to specific moral problems (the goal of the first approach) or whether they are limited to giving a general account of morality that does not itself lead to these specific answers (the method of the second approach). Dewey himself had rejected both alternatives: the first in an attack on the conception of theory that underlies casuistry in the article "Moral Theory and Practice" (1891),[12] and the second in the remainder of the article on T. H. Green cited in the previous paragraph. What was there left for him to do? Dewey replies

> The difficulty, then, is to find the place intermediate between a theory general to the point of abstractness, a theory which provides no help to action, and a theory which attempts to further action but does so at the expense of its spontaneity and breadth. I do not know of any theory, however, which is quite consistent to either point of view."[13]

What would such a theory be like? This question engenders three additional problems in the form of questions. The three questions in turn indicate the subject matter for Dewey's three-course, yearlong, sequence in ethical theory that he taught at the University of Chicago from 1895 to 1902.

The fall quarter course in the Logic of Ethics, including the set of lectures to follow, starts with the question, How do you explain the distinction between the factual and the ethical? "What is the relation of the ethical view of the world to the physical view?" (§1). The question arises because Dewey is starting to develop a new approach to ethical inquiry.[14] This theory must provide some moral guidance, that is, it must have an instrumental function. But it cannot find this guidance in something "beyond" the activity of life.[15] What, then, do we mean by moral guidance when it does not appeal to an ideal that is in some sense outside of or beyond actual life? Is it not obvious that such a standard is required, since the life process as such is both good and evil?

Although there are no extant notes for Dewey's 1896 Winter Quarter course in the Psychology of Ethics, we can gauge the content of the course from the lecture notes to the 1898 "Lectures on Psychological Ethics" and the 1901 "Lectures on the Psychology of Ethics." The central question for these lectures is, How can we give an account of the moral personality, or person capable of dealing with a problematic situation through reconstruction of himself, as a dynamic and self-reconstructing subject, whose experiences include the environment in which they take place? Here, personality becomes an instrument of initiation, which uses intelligence to locate a stimulus (that is, discover a successful hypothesis) and which restores continuity to the life process. Dewey rejects the idealist view that life is a process of working towards a fixed self to be realized.

A person is a dynamic self in a continuous process of reconstruction. Intelligence replaces will as the central category of the moral life. The task is to develop an account of intelligence as a vehicle of reconstruction.

The course in Political Ethics (later called Social Ethics in 1901) deals with the social process as giving dynamic content to experience, including the human activities and interactions that take place within it. This social process, with its economic, political, and moral aspects, is both obstacle and means to the resolution of human problems. The key question is how to find a way to use the process as means or instrument rather than as obstacle. As we will see in Part Two of this book, the 1896 "Lectures on Political Ethics" give Dewey's reconstruction of the alleged antagonisms between the supposedly independent disciplines of Politics, Economics, and Ethics, which, if the theorists are correct, put these disciplines at odds with each other and stand in the way of progress.

A New Logic to Bridge the Dualism
Between Scientific and Moral Inquiry

It is obvious that the Logic of Ethics plays a central role in the construction of an instrumentalist ethics. However, overshadowing the development of this program lies the objection that a moral theory that links moral ideals with practice must acknowledge that some persons and organizations hold to matter-of-fact, working ideals that are not true moral ideals. It seems, then, that the effort to link the ideal and the practical leads to an unsolvable dilemma. Dewey's criticism of empiricist and intuitionalist attempts to explain the "logic of the [moral] categories" (§140) illustrates why.

The empiricist starts with observation and comparison of special cases and develops a general principle, for example, that certain experiences lead to pain and others to pleasure (§141). The difficulty here is that observation and classification require an implicit ideal or standard of value, a "rational factor which directs it," while "denying its existence" (§143, 144, 145). There is no point in holding that the maximizing of pleasure and the avoidance of pain is a principle of selection, unless you already hold that it is your implicit moral ideal. Moreover, the application of a moral ideal leads either to an unscientific uncertainty or a fixed rigidity. Either you must re-evaluate the commandment not to murder in every instance, where murder is a live option, or take it for granted that "an inherited moral code of race and nation" sets the standard (§146).

In summary, empiricism must include every inherited belief of the race and/or nation as moral or take for granted a moral ideal not established on moral grounds. By contrast, the intuitionalist can appeal to "general and universal truth, not particular or contingent. . . . There must then be a power of the mind to realize the universal truths which transcend the particular [experience]" (§150). These truths are in effect axioms. The difficulty here is to avoid a starting point that "will not be truistic" by trying to derive a particular truth from general truths. But "no one ever did this" (§154). There is also a problem concerning "how to subsume the particular under the general" without being "forced to make . . . intuitions more and more general" (§157). In other words, intuitionalism cannot deal with particular cases. In Kant's moral philosophy, the attempt to sustain a general moral ideal apart from the particular facts of life leads to vacuous, general intuitions, such as the view that "the only intuition is that of obligation in general" (§157).

So the empiricist begs the question by assuming a moral ideal that is not discoverable by induction. We are left to conclude that an empirical survey of actual ideals would include some ideals that are not truly moral. The proposed solution is to take the intuitionalist route and locate universal and objective moral principles that can be applied in particular cases. But this effort to get above and beyond particular experience leads us to general principles that fail to provide guidance. There is no way to link the practical with the ideal. An empirical survey of working or *de facto* ideals will include some ideals we want to reject. We can avoid this result by appealing to universal principles, but they will be so abstract that they fail to guide us.

This is the "felt difficulty" Dewey referred to. How does Dewey "locate" and "define" the problem? Since his criticism of intuitionalism has illustrated that we cannot draw a particular truth from a general truth, the demand is to find "a use of the general with regard to the particular as to organize the latter into a comprehensive whole" (§155). To do this we must use the experimental process, not the empirical.

> The experimental process should not be confounded with the empirical process; for the former sets up a unity and by it controls the empirical process. On the other hand this unity which the experimental process asserts is not a fixed thing. It is not asserted for itself but as a working hypothesis for the organization of the empirical process. This method is beyond and below both [empiricist and intuitionalist] systems. The true logic is the logic of an experimental idealism. (§160)

It is difficult to overestimate the importance of this argument. Traditional ethical theory relies upon either inductive or deductive reasoning, and both fail. Reconstruction, that is to say, dealing with the difficulty, requires a new logic of inquiry. This cannot be a logic of moral inquiry or "moral reasoning" as something apart from scientific reasoning. Such a logic would only sustain the gap between the moral and the factual. Nor will it do to reduce or explain moral reasoning as a variety of empirical logic, since that would not provide a true moral ideal.

> There can be no opposition between the categories of objective experience and the categories of moral experience. On the one side is the contention that Ethics is a deductive *a priori* science, essentially at least a psychological science. On the other, that it is an historical inductive science, or at least it is a purely sociological science. One or the other of these presumptions underlies almost every treatise on the science of ethics. (§161)[16]

The "location of the problem" is attained through the development of an experimental logic of inquiry to be shared by scientific and moral inquirers alike, which explains the difference between the scientific and the moral without creating an "opposition" between them. This is the task Dewey undertakes at the beginning of these lectures.

The Program of the Lectures

As previously stated, the lectures begin with the question, "What is the relation of the ethical view of the world to the physical view of the world?" (§1). Their starting point is the apparent "antithesis" or "dualism" between these two views as given in the expressions "physical causation vs. teleological causation; necessity vs. freedom; fact vs. ideal element; is vs. ought" (§2). How do we dissolve this dualism? Dewey takes the position that "Every man must assert the unity of human experience." Further, since physical and biological sciences have "gotten methods that have worked so well, it is inevitable that they should be introduced in ethical and social phenomena" (§3). What is going on in statements such as these? How is Dewey going to explain the factual/moral distinction without lapsing back into dualism, yet still provide for a scientific treatment of morality?

The assertion, "Every man must assert the unity of human experience," appears to refer to the language we all share as a common "organ of communication," as "associated or objective mind."[17] The ordinary judgment is the expression of this association. "Chalk is white," "Water is H_2O," "Getting more exercise is a good thing to do," and "I ought to work harder at my math assignment" are all judgments. They share in common the fact that they are made by persons with regard to some factor or factors in their ongoing experience. All, except for the last (which replaces the copula 'is' with the verb 'ought'), have a subject, copula, and predicate.

So then, the study of judgments in the generic sense represents an attempt to find a common ground for both moral and scientific statements. "Back of the ethical inquiry is the inquiry into the nature of judgment" (§1). "Examination has not gone far enough back" (§4). Here Dewey pursues a strategy he had first worked out in his February 1892 "Introduction to Philosophy: Syllabus of Course 5."[18] Whenever you confront an apparently inexplicable dualism you need to "get back of it."[19]

> There are two ways of going at the problem. One is to simply take it and try to solve it. This never gives satisfactory results in philosophy. . . . The point is to get back of the problem and find the source of it. The problem then disappears. Here as everywhere the question is, how does this problem arise? (§50)

Later, following his own analysis of judgment, Dewey asserts that "The present standpoint which we have reached solves the problem by dissolving it" (§60). How then does the problem of discontinuity between scientific language and moral language arise? How do we "locate" this problem? How does Dewey "dissolve" this problem and pave the way for the link between scientific and moral inquiry that he refers to in 1903 as a "scientific treatment of morality"?

Here is a sketch of Dewey's answer to these questions, given as a prelude to his own analysis of judgment. First, how does the problem come about?

> We have isolated the intellectual judgment from its place in experience as a whole. It has been isolated both on the side of its origin and of its purpose. We have not asked what it evolves from nor what its function, purpose, is. (§51)

> The judgment represents the phases of the evaluation of experience. It is the process by which one value is changed for another value. (§52)

> Neither does the judgment originate of itself from strictly logical considerations, but from the defect or break-down of some previous value. "Caesar crosses the Rubicon." The real significance of this is found neither in the subject nor predicate, but in the total idea of Caesar who made the advance to destroy the old decaying Republic. (§53)

> As long as we are making out the judgment or familiarizing ourselves with it, the two elements of subject and predicate stand out as separate, but afterwards the value is a single idea in the mind. This value is the true copula, e.g., a new element in the air, [a] theory of evolution. (§54)

The reader familiar with Dewey will recognize these assertions as elements in his logic of inquiry. But what do the assertions have to do with the problem of the discontinuity or dualism between the scientific and the moral?

It is helpful at this point to consider two influential examples of the isolation Dewey refers to in the quotations just cited. In developing his famous argument that "good is not to be considered a natural object," G. E. Moore asserts "there is no meaning in saying that pleasure is good, unless good is something different than pleasure." To think that good means the same thing as pleasure is to commit the "naturalistic fallacy" or fallacy of confusing good with some "natural object."[20] The evidence that this really is a fallacy is found in what later philosophers called "the open question argument." That is, if we are entertaining the view "that pleasure is good" or that any other thing in nature is good, we need only ask, "is pleasure (or whatever it may be) after all good?" and we will see that we are not asking whether pleasure is pleasant. Through this process we recognize that pleasure is a "distinct entity" and that it is not the same thing as good.[21]

Similarly, take H. A. Prichard's criticism of utilitarianism in his well-known essay, "Does Moral Philosophy Rest on a Mistake?" The utilitarian's attempt to base obligation upon happiness presupposes two links: (1) "that what is good ought to be," and (2) "the apprehension that something good which is not an action ought to be involves just the feeling of imperativeness or obligation which is to be aroused by the thought of the action which will originate it." Prichard concludes instead that "The word 'ought' refers to actions and actions alone."[22]

The significance of these two arguments with regard to Dewey's discussion of judgment is that both Moore and Prichard take judgments as such, without regard to their origin, and ignore the fact that they are made within a process of inquiry. When they are taken as judgments as such rather than as distinctions that play a functional role within the inquiry, it is hard for anyone to find any connection between them, and an apparent dualism is the result.[23] According to Moore, the judgment "Pleasure is good" does not make sense, so the only way to explain the truth in the proposition is create a dualism between the non-natural or "good" aspects of the judgment and the natural or "pleasure" aspect of the judgment. The possibility that the judgment is a response to this tension and is an hypothesis in action does not occur to Moore. Similarly, Prichard starts with a judgment such as "It is good to promote happiness" and finds no connection between this judgment and obligation judgments. If there is to be any connection at all between "It is good to promote happiness," and "We ought to promote happiness," it is because we hold that "What is good ought to be." But, properly speaking, the word 'ought', as in the judgment "You ought to do X," refers to actions and actions alone. It does not occur to Prichard that the latter judgment is already about good in the sense that it is a phase in our response to a situation that requires valuation, so that there is a continuity between goods and oughts.[24]

The way we account for the terms in our moral judgments has an import far greater than the technical-professional concerns of philosophers. These judgments and the terms they employ play a functional role in dealing with the problems of life. For example, take Dewey's comments on the "temperance reform" movement.

> Here is a certain waste of social powers, resulting in crime and poverty. This constitutes a reflection on the friction. The definiteness with which the ideal is conceived will be exactly correlative with the definiteness with which the facts are perceived. Friction itself sets up this polarity of movement. If you abstract a phase of the facts, the ideal becomes equally partial. If you abstract simply [the] act of alcohol or poison, your ideal is to do away with it. If the perception of facts is extended to poorly housed, overworked people, the ideal will be extended to amelioration of their condition. The conception will become a working hypothesis with reference to which facts are gathered thereafter, either of crime, etc., for the prohibitionist, or of industrial conditions for the person interested in social and industrial reform. (§182)

These remarks illustrate how the traditional theory of judgment that Dewey criticizes in the lectures leads us to the separation of the factual and the moral and how the use of the judgment as a hypothesis will restore that continuity. Moore's separation of good from fact and scientific inquiry, and Prichard's separation of ought from good are examples of separations that influence the way in which we formulate the moral problem! They illustrate Dewey's assertion (see §51) that we have isolated the intellectual judgment from its place in the whole. The outcome of the separation in the case of ethical theory is the further separation of moral judgments from intellectual judgments about facts. Once you do this, the subject matter of moral inquiry concerns the truth of moral judgments, taken as such. You will take note of the fact of drinking and its effects and then try to justify a moral judgment such as "people ought to stop drinking alcohol" or "alcohol ought to be abolished." In terms of more contemporary problems, you will concern yourself with such judgments as "Abortion ought (ought not) to be abolished," "We ought (ought not) to put more money in the public schools," or "We ought (ought not) to establish affirmative action polices."

The point is not that we should ignore such proposals, so long as they are regarded as responses to problems. The task is to explore the context of morally problematic situations in order to gain a better understanding about what has to be done in order to deal with them. Dewey asks

> How can the ordinary ideal of justice help in the application of justice to industrial trusts? One must first find the trend of industrial force. There must be some theory of interpretation, a theory of ethical movement of society as a whole as an ethical organization. And we must see what the relation of this movement is

to the whole organism. This requires patience, so it seems easier to do something at once. (§190)

Mainstream moral theory encourages us to "do something at once" and develop the ordinary conception of justice in order to find a justified way to condemn the trusts. This conception of the task of theory makes no room, *qua* theory, for the person who is working out a way to deal with the problems that the trusts present.

In a later discussion of his "experimental idealist" reconstruction of the notion of perfection, Dewey asserts that "practically, the determination of the best in the concrete calls forth the greatest moral energy, while the attempt to attain to the abstract perfection is vague and unsatisfactory" (§234). The justification of a statement such as "the trusts ought to be abolished" is abstract in the sense in which Dewey uses the term. Granted that the directive appears to be specific, it ignores the problem of dealing with the opposition that would inevitably occur when anyone attempts to do it.[25] Dewey's *The Study of Ethics: A Syllabus* (1894) brings up the belief in "fixed," "absolute," and "ready-made" ideals.

> No moral value attaches to their working-out, or formation. It may belong to the attitude taken towards them, to their choice or rejection, but nothing more. But, in our actual experience, no such separation exists between forming and choosing an end of action. Our moral discipline consists even more in the responsibility put upon us to develop ideals, than in choosing between them when made. The making of plans, working them out into their bearings, etc., is at once a test of character and a factor in building it up.[26]

The logical basis for the emphasis Dewey places upon working out ideals is found in his discussion of the copula in the ordinary judgment. Therefore, we turn to this discussion next.

But first, here is a brief summary of his account of the dynamic function of the copula. "The nature of action is such as to distinguish itself into the means of action [predicate or 'immediate'] on the one side and method of action [subject or 'mediate'] on the other" (§60). "How does experience 'sweet sugar' get translated into this other idea 'Sugar is sweet'?" (§62). "There must be resistance," "some opposition" (§61, 63). For example, "The sugar is out of reach." "The visual activity is overflowing into the touch and taste centers. The mouth waters even though the sugar has not been tasted" (§63). Then, "through this resistance the subject and predicate are set off from each other" (§64). In this process, "the copula is always ultimately an act which comprehends the fact [sugar] and idea [sweet]" (§5). "The contradiction which the rationalist and idealist fall into is caused by the failure to see that judgment is not completed until realized. The realization is the copula which has absorbed into itself both subject and predicate" (§56). The next step is to show how the dynamic copula is a common factor in all judgments, including the intellectual, the aesthetic, and the moral.[27]

Intellectual, Aesthetic, and Moral Judgments

Discussion in the previous section began with the problem of the relation of the ethical view of the world to the physical. More specifically, "science seems to eliminate the self" (§114), that is, the subject matter of morality. Given the "apparent disjunction of the actual and ideal, . . . the testing point of every ethical system is how it accounts for the splitting up of the ethical experience into the 'is' and of the 'might be'" (§171). How do we solve this problem? As just stated, the subject, copula, and predicate are common factors in moral, intellectual, and (as we will shortly see) aesthetic judgments. Tension is another common factor in all three judgments. "The intellectual interest is in proper sphere of the tension. The ethical interest is in arresting the tension—the intellectual interest—at a certain point and turning it to some practical end" (§92). The aesthetic interest is a "plot interest," an interest "not now in the fact of tension but in the self as comprehending or containing the tension" (§94).

These three factors will be discussed shortly, but it is important first to discuss an issue that Dewey appears to gloss over in these lectures and elsewhere. In §117, he asserts that "this setting off of this world of objects and laws with which science deals over against moral experience, is itself a phase in the development of experience as practical or moral."[28] An ambiguity develops because much of Dewey's discussion marks out the contrast between intellectual and moral judgments—or so at least the reader is inclined to take it. If so, there are then two types of moral judgments: (1) primitive or basic morality as any attempt to control practical experience and (2) the moral *qua* moral as expressed in the moral judgments that constitute the subject matter of ethical theory. The first type is found in the familiar pragmatic instrumentalist judgment that all thought is practical in the sense that it is a response to the problematic, and the second is found in the view that actual moral judgments such as "X is good" or "X ought to be done" are contrasted with factual judgments such as "Chalk is white."

This argument is tempting, but incorrect, and Dewey himself eventually realized it could get him into trouble. The view arises because we tend to think of inquiry as a temporal sequence. First, we have tension, a practical problem that we call "moral". Second, we distinguish two aspects of this problem, the scientific and the moral in a second sense of the term (as moral *qua* moral). According to Dewey, the initial tension is the stimulus for and guide to all further inquiry. Since this initial tension is practical, i.e., it is a question about what to do, we come to the conclusion that all further inquiry is governed by the individual's practical interest. Then our moral interest in the second sense is controlled by our practical interest, that is, our basic moral interest in the first sense. But this is unsatisfactory, so it is necessary for some other moral theorist who is not an instrumentalist to supply us with a sense of morality that is not based upon our practical interest.

But in a 1922 article, Dewey asserts that his account of the "steps" in a complete act of thought is "formal." "It is a matter of indifference which [step] comes first."[29] Apply this insight to our current discussion, and the distinction between the factual and the moral arises in an effort to deal with the problem, either actual or anticipated. To say we start with a practical problem that is also a moral problem in the first sense, and then at some later time we go on to characterize it as an intellectual problem or a moral qua moral problem, is mistaken. The distinctions between the moral, the factual, and the aesthetic are, in Dewey's language, "abstractions" that are put forth as part of a logical process in locating, characterizing, and dealing with the tension (§92). "These three values are not three things. They are simply names which we give to one process according to the stage at which we take it" (§94). The expression "one process" is crucial. There is no process of first locating the problem as practical, and then going on to discuss the intellectual, aesthetic, and moral values to be determined as part of the practical problem. The problem is practical through and through. The distinctions are made within the "one process" as phases of our response to a practical problem already characterized as such, which we then try to resolve by intellectual or moral means, or some combination of both.[30] This is the most plausible account of Dewey's position.

It will be objected that if the practical interest is present throughout the "one process" of experience, then this practical interest is essentially selfish and hence nonmoral or even immoral. But the objection misses a subtle aspect of Dewey's analysis. He is asserting that the moral interest reflects a distinction made within experience, not, as the objection implies, a distinction made in opposition to experience in order to thwart it. That may seem a trivial point, but it leads us to shift interest to the stimuli that restore continuity of function to experience, rather than a selfish "self" that operates over against the moral self. The effort shifts the whole emphasis in moral inquiry to an experimental or "inquiry" function instead of trying to seek out a justification for morality over against self-interest. The inquiry aspect involves proposals to reconstruct experience so as to bring about a new experience, and the experimental aspect involves the testing of proposals in action. This pursuit requires no justification other than the fact that the occurrence of the conflict situation serves as the starting point for the use of intelligence, which will lead to activities that remove the obstacle.

The three phases of experience that we refer to as intellectual, aesthetic, and moral can be briefly characterized.

1. *Intellectual Interest.* Stated negatively, the "tension is not felt to be in and of the self in its deepest sense." "It is not realized that the tension is actually the outcome of the self, the doings of the self" (§90). In other words, the interest is in what takes place, without regard to your own interest in the outcome.[31] Yet it is guided by a purpose which also is a "fact of itself" which mediates this intellectual interest. For example, when a person is making a watch, "this thought of the purpose gives the criterion for the correctness of the parts and their adjustment with each other" (§91). In sum, intellectual inquiry, particularly scientific inquiry, "seems to eliminate self" (§114), but it in fact only ignores self and leaves out the activities of the inquirer as subject matter for inquiry.

2. *Aesthetic Interest.* Here, "the tension and the solution of the tension are both felt within the self's own experience." Unlike the intellectual judgment, "interest is not now in the fact of tension but in the self as comprehending or containing the tension. 'Self' here means total experience. The problem interest becomes the plot interest" (§94). The aesthetic interest is a kind of harbinger of the moral interest, as indicated by Greek art (§103). "The aesthetic is the regnant idea in philosophy" (§107). Although "the process of experience is assumed . . . the struggle as a struggle always falls outside of the aesthetic experience" (§105).

3. *Moral Interest.* The interest in and for the self as a process of experience in tension is assumed. "The moral antagonism is the setting up of one thing against another in action" (§93). "A new tension of a different kind—not between objects as objects [as in the intellectual interest] but between a thing and a standard, between a habit and a particular case—is now set up" (§102). "The limitation of the intellectual experience was that it was interested in the fact of the tension, the material [including the self] being presupposed. . . . In the moral experience the material belongs to the self, just as much as the process of dealing with the material. The subject is the sense object" (§104).

Why should we accept this account? Why is it given in such abstract language?

The answer to the second question is easiest. We are to regard these definitions as hypotheses.

> The process of definition is a process of securing the accurate and economical and efficient conditions and stimuli to activity. (§117)

> The only attempted verification of these hypotheses, here, is that they give unity to our experience. It shows how problems have arisen and how we may get rid of them. (§118)

The answer to the first question is more difficult. Recall the problem Dewey had posed earlier: to find a "place intermediate" between a theory that is so abstract it provides no help to action and "a theory which attempts to further action but does so at the expense of spontaneity and breadth."[32] Suppose for the sake of further discussion that Dewey is trying to dissolve this problem by reconstructing the function of abstraction. Instead of searching for a definition of morality that will turn out to be too abstract to guide us, or a set of specific rules that are simply to be followed and hence eliminate all spontaneity, the function of abstraction is to enable us to find a way to deal with the tensions and problematic situations that arise in experience. The abstractions are to be used as instruments. How does he work this out?

In §104, Dewey discusses the "moral experience." "The subject is the sense object. The predicate is the law or statement. . . . The predicate is the law as regulative or normative." Later he asserts that "the movement from the subject to the predicate sets up the ideal or aim" (§137). What does this mean, and how does it come about? Consider a person who judges "Y is good." The subject of these judgments are the actions and activities of the individual as a subject matter to be investigated. Suppose a certain tension occurs in experience that is at first unconscious, but which eventually leads this individual to mark off a new value (§134). Taken by itself, the individual's activity is an expression of "established habits and life," but taken socially the individual works within "institutions and structure already formed." Then the predicate "is good" expresses the "future side, the end worked for rather than the acquired law [or habit]." The self or individual is both subject and predicate in tension. "Every moral experience reduces itself ultimately to the problem of unifying ideals with these established habits and life" (§136).

So far then, the ideal is not outside the self, but it is an expression of the development of tension within the self—the conflict between existing habits and the ideal set forth. When the tension is resolved, the "antagonism" disappears, and we have "the realized moral experience," including the good, the bad (or older, habitual self), and responsibility (§139). How does this realized experience come about? The answer, from the standpoint of the individual, involves the detailed operation of desire, habit, impulse, and intelligence, including the use of the intellectual judgment. The process is experimental and the solution has to be worked out and tested in action. The answer, on the social side, is that "power is conditioned by [an] end" (§138). By contrast, Utopian or revolutionary anarchism sets up "an end which is out of relation to the present power" (§138). The success of the end is a function of available operating conditions.

To return to our question about the instrumental function of this account, full recognition of this function requires that we take for granted (at least for purposes of discussion) the standpoint that we make distinctions within experience in order to deal with problematic situations that arise within it.[33] So regarded, intellectual, aesthetic, and moral judgments are "stages" in a single process of experience that is itself moral in that the individual is required to make choices and judgments with regard to the disposition of his or her own activity. The distinction between individual and social is also made in response to tension within experience. Experience is not cut off from the world. But, within experience, we can distinguish the point of view of the individual, as an active initiator who deals with this tension, from the role of the environment as both obstacle in producing the tension and means in the carrying out of ends set forth by the individual.[34]

These considerations establish a starting point for further inquiry with regard to the resolution of tensions within experience. The lectures are an invitation to develop a more concrete account of the means to deal with problematic situations. As we have already noted, Dewey does this in the "Lectures on Psychological Ethics" and the "Lectures on Political Ethics" that he gave in his regular course sequence following the "Lectures on the Logic of Ethics," as well as many other books that came later. Most important for our purposes is Dewey's reconstruction of moral inquiry so that the reconstruction of experience becomes an integral part of this inquiry. No longer is the moral philosopher content to give an explanation and/or justification of morality while leaving the "working out" of morality to some other discipline or person. Moral inquiry is concerned with the "working out" of a response to the problematic; the moral inquirer becomes involved in a practical task.

To illustrate, consider the discussion of "the logic of the formation of ideals" in chapter 10 of the lectures. At certain critical points, experience requires reconstruction and readjustment.

> The distinction between the ideal and the actual arises out of and because of this
> necessity of reconstruction. Something now has to be done because of the accumulated details. Except at these times the ideal is actualized and there can be

no split. The split arises because, when these accumulations become so numerous, it is necessary to reflect. . . .The stopping to think is the actual thinking. When friction arises it is a sign that you should stop and reflect. (§176)

Further, "When we reflect upon experience as a whole and set before us objectively a certain state of things the subject drops out. There is projection on one side and withdrawal on the other" (§178). Dewey gives the example of a student who is graduating and "there is a consciousness of something ahead with reference to which he must use his resources." There is a tension between accomplished or habitual self and a "sense of work yet to be done" (§179). This in effect is the "withdrawal" or stopping for reflection phase of experience. The projection phase involves the formation of the ideal.

The life impulse never stops. So long as there is no friction, there is no sense of a break; but if friction occurs, a person feels that what has been accomplished is an obstacle to what should be accomplished. The life process is the permanent thing. "As the actual side becomes defined as an object, the impulse side becomes defined as an ideal" (§180).

In this process, an ideal "is not an object to be realized. It is a method of activity and not a thing" (§186). "The term 'ideal' may be changed to 'plan,' and this appears clearer. When we have a plan, it seems to mark the outline of our activity . . . sets certain channels, preferred to others, along which the activity is to flow, and allows one to economize his effort" (§196).

This exposition invites an objection that, if unanswered, would show the fundamental inadequacy in Dewey's approach to ethical inquiry as outlined thus far. As indicated above, his discussion is based upon the notion of language as a shared or unifying factor in human experience. The copula is the dynamic connecting link between the particular ideal and the moral universal. The judgment "X is good" is a plan for action put forth by an individual. The objection is that Dewey fails to consider judgments of the form "X ought to be done," where the copula "ought" expresses some different relation than a plan for action. The plan is self-centered and fails to capture our sense of obligation to others. But Dewey does not discuss the concept of obligation in these lectures, and, when he does discuss it in his 1900 "Lectures on the Logic of Ethics," the idea of duty is characterized in terms of a more pronounced sense of the tension between ideal and actual.[35]

How are we to evaluate this objection? No final answer will be attempted here, but two observations are in order. The first gives some support for the objection, and the second suggests that it misses the point because it ignores the social control within the situation in which the plan for action is made.

First, in §241, Dewey discusses the relationship of the concepts of good and bad to the concepts of right and wrong. He regards the two sets of concepts as variations of "one and the same category." Both are linked with the evaluation and satisfaction of impulse, but the good is more general, while the right pertains to the satisfaction of a particular impulse. This analysis does not seem to me to be convincing or even very clear. Later, in §256, he discusses rightness in terms of one person's interests overlapping another's. "While he has his standard, other people have their standards and force theirs upon him by their actions toward him." Yet this *de facto* conflict is regarded as "a conflict between himself as an isolated end and himself as a social end." The implication appears to be that the notion of "himself as a social end" refers to some ideal self that is not really himself in any working or functional sense. But this is the same defect Dewey attributed to T. H. Green.

In 1930, Dewey modified his earlier standpoint on the relation between good and right. He asserted that the notion of right and obligation has a different origin than that of individual good. Obligations develop because it is a normal part of experience for individuals to make demands upon each other. These conflict, and so we develop a system of demands that are generally accepted.[36] This account avoids the appeal to the "ideal self," yet, taken as such, it is not instrumental in the quest for shared obligations.

Second, we can accept this later reconstruction of Dewey's thought yet continue to employ the standpoint presented in these lectures. There already is some unity in our life experience. We speak a common language. It is taken for granted that we already "get along" with others to some extent. The social aspect of experience, as developed in the "Lectures on Political Ethics" presented in Part Two, provides a common core of professions and institutions that are roughly coordinated with each other. Throughout the 1890s, Dewey accepted the notion of the organic character of society (but not the view that society is a ready made, complete organism) as a tool for dealing with social conflict. These points are not in dispute. But what is called for is an account of obligation that provides guidance with regard to the disputes that do occur.

Recall again that Dewey is trying to avoid an approach to moral inquiry that is so mechanical and casuistic it destroys all spontaneity in life, while also avoiding an approach so abstract as to give no help to action. Late in the lectures, Dewey makes an assertion that spontaneity cannot be suppressed in any event. "The feeling that one ought not to act until he can see that good is guaranteed hampers action. The element of faith or spontaneity cannot be eliminated" (§249). If this is correct—and certainly Dewey's characterization of the active character of the learner in his educational theory is a sustained argument for this position—the problem before us changes significantly. The moral control we have been searching for cannot come from fixed, and hence inhibiting, moral principles. In Dewey's view, it must come from the situation itself, both in its psychological and social aspects.[37] This situation must be limiting yet open. The "Lectures on Political Ethics" in Part Two address the social aspect of the situation as an element of social control.

Religious Experience

In §112, Dewey speaks of the religious phase of experience in relation to the intellectual, aesthetic, and moral experience.

> The phase of the experience known as the religious is any one of the others taken adequately and not abstracted. It is not a fourth thing. It is any one of these realized adequately, taken as a phase of the whole, and therefore having the meaning of the whole taken back into it. Any experience which can demand the whole devotion of the being is religious. It is closer to one than to another.

In addition, chapter 6 is devoted to rejection of the separation between the individual and God. In §262, he asserts that "The effort to change conditions is the only moral judgment. The external condemnation is but self-congratulation. This is the teaching of Christ."

Steven C. Rockefeller has given us a thorough account of the development of Dewey's religious thought.[38] At the time of the lectures given here, it is obvious that Dewey is reconstructing Christianity to do away with the dualisms he finds in popular versions of the doctrine. Two additional points stand out here as well. First, although Dewey asserts that the religious experience is not to be separated from other experience, that is, it is not a "fourth thing," the experience does seem to be unique in the sense that it is not, so far as the reader can tell, a response to a tension or problematic situation, but is, rather, a product of grace, a happenstance. In other words, there is no suggestion that we can set forth initiatives that will result in religious experience.

Second, there is a sense in which the lectures, taken as a whole, appear to be an attempt to do what apparently can't be done. The guiding theme of "unity" that pervades the entire lectures appears to be an effort to realize this unity in his own experience and presumably in the experience of his listeners as well.

Notes

1. For the premier importance of the problematic and the problematic situation in Dewey's theory of inquiry, see his *Logic: The Theory of Inquiry* (1938), *LW*, 12:3, and especially pp. 41–42, for a restatement of this standpoint in the language of the organism-

environment distinction that is, historically, the starting point for his account of inquiry. On the latter point, see Dewey's "Reply to Albert G. A. Balz" (1949), *LW*, 16:280–94, especially p. 288.

The term 'problematic situation' does not appear in either set of the lectures given in this volume, yet it is clear that he had the notion if not this exact form of expression. For example, in this volume, see the "Lectures on the Logic of Ethics," §2, 50, 60, and especially 89 and 110; and in the "Lectures on Political Ethics," see §169.

2. The lectures are written in the language of T. H. Green, F. H. Bradley, and Bernard Bosanquet. Herbert W. Schneider has asserted that Dewey "used [this] language of objective idealism to direct evolutionary thought against its conclusions" (cited by John Herman Randall in his article, "The Future of John Dewey's Philosophy," *Journal of Philosophy* 56 [December 1959]: 1007). It is natural to question this strategy, because the idealist movement is a relic of the past and will probably never be revived. Yet, it is difficult to imagine Dewey using the language of the mainstream utilitarian and Kantian traditions, since they are saturated with the dualisms of mind/body, moral/factual, etc., that he is trying to reject. Objective idealism provides a more congenial starting point.

There is a good account of Dewey's relation to Hegel and T. H. Green in Alan Ryan, *John Dewey and the High Tide of American Liberalism* (New York: W. W. Norton, 1995), pp. 89–96. Ryan contrasts Green's "good natured and cooperative society of liberal-minded progressives" with Hegel's emphasis upon the need for cultural conflict and war, and guesses that Dewey played down the latter. But see Dewey's 1898 "Lectures on Political Ethics," *LPPE*, pp. 449–50, for an account of the evolution of rights through conflict.

3. In his 1948 introduction to a reprint of *Reconstruction in Philosophy* (*MW*, vol. 12, 1921), Dewey refers to a "movement" towards a "new moral order." Yet "the specific reconstructions that are involved in this carrying on to fulfillment . . . we have as yet attained only partially," and "even a satisfactory listing of the issues that are involved with respect to philosophy must, by and large, wait till the philosophic movement in this direction has been carried beyond any point as yet attained" (*MW*, 12:275–76). The neglect of Dewey's thought as an instrument of inquiry, despite an immense and continuing philosophical interest in specific moral issues in the last twenty-five years, suggests that this "philosophic movement" has not taken place.

4. References in this paragraph are to Dewey's *Logic*, *LW*, 12:9, 527, 123–41.

5. For example, Alan Ryan's treatment of Dewey's ethics, politics, art, and religion tries to "evade technical questions about Dewey's logic and theory of truth" (Ryan, *John Dewey*, 35). Ryan seems to take it for granted that Dewey's ethics and politics can be studied apart from his theory of inquiry. Robert Westbrook makes only cursory reference to Dewey's major 1903 essay, "Logical Conditions of a Scientific Treatment of Morality" (*MW*, 3:3–39). See Robert Westbrook, *John Dewey and American Democracy* (Ithaca: Cornell University Press, 1991), pp. 144–45. This essay was originally published in a University of Chicago publication, *Investigations Representing the Departments, Part II: Philosophy, Education*, designed to give an accounting of work in the various departments. The effort to construct a "scientific treatment" of morality is primarily based upon

Dewey's course in the Logic of Ethics. Steven C. Rockefeller refers to the "function of logical principles and concepts in [the] experimental process," but does not relate this to ethical inquiry. See his *John Dewey: Religious Faith and Democratic Humanism* (New York: Columbia University Press, 1991), p. 542. Ernest Nagel's introduction to the Southern Illinois Press edition of *Logic: The Theory of Inquiry* indicates the relevance of the logic of inquiry for moral questions, but does not develop the point further. See *LW*, 12:vii, and p. x note. Nagel recognized that "Dewey wrote his *Logic* to help the social sciences progress at the same pace as the natural sciences . . . that an appropriate logic should be an organon for the solution of pressing social problems." For more on this, see also Patrick Suppes, "Nagel's Lectures on Dewey's Logic," in *Philosophy, Science, and Scientific Method: Essays in Honor of Ernest Nagel* (New York: St. Martin's Press, 1969), p. 3. According to Suppes, Nagel emphasized Dewey's view that moral evaluations "contain overt transformations" or reconstructions, as opposed to the classical view that they reflect "predetermined and given ends in themselves" (14–15). Jennifer Welchman's *Dewey's Ethical Thought* (Ithaca: Cornell University Press, 1995) acknowledges the influence of Bradley's logic upon Dewey, but does not pursue the matter further. Chapters 5 and 6 are noteworthy for their attempt to show the continuity between Dewey's 1902–1903 essays on the logic of ethical inquiry and the covertly experimental approach taken in the first edition (1908) of Dewey's *Ethics* (co-written with James H. Tufts), see *MW*, vol. 5. Perhaps the best treatment of ethical inquiry as controlled by Dewey's logic of inquiry is given in James Campbell's *Understanding John Dewey: Nature and Cooperative Intelligence* (Chicago: Open Court, 1995), pp. 110–23.

6. See Dewey's contribution to *Studies in Logical Theory* (1903), *MW*, 2:295–375, especially Sections 2, 3 and 4, which has a bearing upon the development of a logic of ethical inquiry, but does not develop it. The reasoning of these lectures reappears in a very abbreviated form in his "Logical Conditions of a Scientific Treatment of Morality" (1903), *MW* 3:3–39, especially Sections 3 and 4. In the former, Dewey asserts that

> All the distinctions discovered within thinking . . . come within the thought-situation as growing out of a characteristic antecedent typical formation of experience; and have for their purpose the solution of the peculiar problem with respect to which the thought function is generated or evolved. (336)

Later in the same work, Dewey asserts that even though "distinctions . . . are genetic and historic," and hence "working or instrumental," we tend to erect them into "rigid and ready-made structural differences of reality" (348). Yet, the working basis for the factual-moral distinction is not discussed in the *Studies*, and then only briefly and without reference to the general theory of judgments in "Logical Conditions" (20–23).

7. Quotations in this paragraph are from *LW*, 5:150–51.

8. The lectures emphasize the "unity" phase of experience. Dewey's later writings emphasize its diversity, contingency, and problematic character. Yet, even these writings contain occasional allusions to the need for unity. Take these remarks, from about 1948, suggesting that *Experience and Culture* is a better title for his 1929 book, *Experience and Nature*.

"Culture" designates, . . . in their reciprocal interconnections, that immense diversity of human affairs, interests, concerns, values which compartmentalists pigeonhole under "religion" "morals" "aesthetics" "politics" "economics" etc. Instead of separating, isolating and insulating the many aspects of a common life, "culture" holds them together in their human and humanistic unity—a service which "experience" has ceased to render. (From the "Unfinished Introduction" to a new edition of *Experience and Nature*, published as Appendix 1 to the reprint in *LW*, 1:363)

There are many other expressions of the sentiment towards unity in Dewey's works, typically at the very end of the work. For example,

every act may carry within itself a consoling and supporting consciousness of the whole to which it belongs and which in some sense belongs to it. With responsibility for the intelligent determination of particular acts may go a joyful emancipation from the burden for responsibility for the whole which sustains them, giving them their final outcome and quality. There is a conceit fostered by perversion of religion which assimilates the universe to our personal desires; but there is also a conceit of carrying the load of the universe from which religion liberates us. Within the flickering inconsequential acts of separate selves dwells a sense of the whole which claims and dignifies them. In its presence we put off mortality and live in the universal. The life of the community in which we live and have our being is the fit symbol of this relationship. The acts in which we express our perception of the ties which bind us to others are its only rites and ceremonies. (*Human Nature and Conduct* [1922], *MW*, 14:227)

We live, as Emerson said, in the lap of an immense intelligence. But that intelligence is dormant, and its communications are broken, inarticulate, and faint until it possesses the local community as its medium. (*The Public and its Problems* [1927], *LW*, 2:372)

A mind that has opened itself to experience and that has ripened through its discipline knows its own littleness and impotencies; it knows that its wishes and acknowledgments are not final measures of the universe whether in knowledge or in conduct, and hence are, in the end, transient. But it also knows that its juvenile assumption of power and achievement is not a dream to be wholly forgotten. It implies a unity with the universe that is to be preserved. (*Experience and Nature*, *LW*, 1:313)

The need for a direction of action in large social fields is the source of a genuine demand for unification of scientific conclusions. They are organized when their bearing on the conduct of life is disclosed. It is at this point that the extraordinary and multifarious results of scientific inquiry are unorganized, scattered, chaotic. The astronomer, biologist, chemist, may attain systematic wholes, at least for a time, within his own field. But when we come to the bearing of special conclusions upon the conduct of social life, we are outside of technical fields, at a loss. The force of tradition and dogmatic authority is due, more than to anything else, to precisely this defect. Man has never had such a varied body of Knowledge in his possession before, and probably never before has he been so uncertain and so perplexed as to what his knowledge means, what it points to in action and in consequences. (*The Quest for Certainty* [1929], *LW*, 4:249)

The first four quotes express our concern about the unity of the whole, while the last expresses the demand to unite the scientific and the moral that is dealt with in the lectures to follow.

9. *MW*, 6:236–37.

10. See vol. 5 of *MW*.

11. Quotations in this and the next paragraph are from Dewey's "Green's Theory of the Moral Motive," *EW*, 3:155.

12. *EW*, 3:93–109. The writers criticized in the article—Felix Adler, Bernard Bosanquet, William M. Salter, and Henry Sidgwick—are not casuists in the sense that they try to develop rigid rules for conduct. Yet, Dewey accuses them of sharing a view of moral theory as "an attempt to find a philosophic 'basis' or foundation for moral activity in something beyond that activity itself." Although these writers do not advocate an "ethical cookbook"—a collection of rules for conduct," they share in common the view that moral knowledge exists outside of human activity (94).

13. *EW*, 3:155.

14. But, this is not an entirely new approach. For Dewey's use of Darwin at this time, see these lectures, §143.

15. In "Moral Theory and Practice," Dewey asserts that

> Moral theory, then, is the analytic perception of the conditions and relations in hand in a given act,—it is the action *in idea*. It is the construction of the act in thought against its outward construction. *It is, therefore, the doing,—the act itself, in its emerging.* So far are we from any divorce of moral theory and practice that theory is the ideal act, and conduct is the executed insight. This is our thesis. (*EW*, 3:95)

Substitute the notion of "plans for action" for the somewhat murky "construction of the act in thought," and "action" for "outward construction," and you are left with the notion that ethical theory has to enact any plan for action, whether it is moral or not. This is hardly the basis for an ethical theory.

16. The expression "at least a psychological science" appears obscure. But recall that the fundamental premise of intuitionalism is that "there must . . . be a power of the mind to realize the universal truths which transcend the particular" (§150). Intuitionalism is always in danger of falling back into psychologism, or the view that these universal truths are really only expressions of emotion or feeling. Dewey's reconstruction of ethical theory will involve the reconstruction of this psychological standpoint implicit in intuitionalism, as well as the reconstruction of the sociological standpoint implicit in empiricism. Hence the disciplines of "Psychological Ethics" and "Social Ethics."

17. See Dewey's 1898 "Lectures on Political Ethics," *LPPE*, pp. 373, 375. The discussion of language as "objective mind" in these lectures (373–79) gives Dewey's version of the identity of thought and language.

18. *EW*, 3:211–35, especially pp. 211–12.

19. A case can be made that Dewey's general philosophical strategy is to treat any apparent dualism by regarding it as a distinction, made within a unity for purposes of dealing with a problematic situation. There is an interesting project for someone who wants to go through his major works to see how he employs this strategy.

20. G. E. Moore, *Principia Ethica* (Cambridge: Cambridge University Press, 1903), pp. 13–14. In his immediately prior discussion of the judgment "pleasure is good," Moore as-

serts that it cannot express (1) that "most people have used the word [good] for what is pleasant," or (2) that when they say "'Pleasure is good' . . . they merely mean 'Pleasure is pleasure'" (11–12). To refer to Dewey's account in these lectures, one alternative for dealing with this difficulty is offered by the empiricist school of logic, but it cannot account for good as a universal (§32). The second alternative is the Kantian position that all judgment is a synthesis of concepts, but this leads only to tautology (§9) or a "purely formal" unity of the various "heterogenous" things asserted in the predicate (§40). The similarity of these two arguments suggest that Moore is aware of Bradley's criticism of ordinary judgments. But, while Dewey builds upon the conclusion of Lotze and Bradley that all "simple" judgments are hypothetical (§22) and applies it to moral judgments, Moore avoids the difficulty by asserting that 'good' refers to "a different kind of object from any which can be moved about." See his discussion of Bradley in *Principia Ethica*, pp. 124–25.

21. Moore, *Principia Ethica*, p. 16.

22. H. A. Prichard, "Does Moral Philosophy Rest on a Mistake?" (1912), reprinted in his *Moral Obligation and Duty and Interest* (London: Oxford University Press, 1968), p. 4. Dewey, following F. H. Bradley, assumes that the basic unit of inquiry is the judgment, not the word. It is interesting to speculate what the history of twentieth-century ethical theory would have been like if mainstream moral philosophers had explored this tradition rather than talking about the meaning of moral terms such as 'good' and 'ought' as if these could be discussed independently of the role they play in the inquiry for which they are employed.

23. For Dewey, this sorting out into different "kinds" of judgments resorts to the practices of definition and classification associated with the outdated account of inquiry presupposed by Aristotlean logic. See chapter 5 of his *Logic, LW*, 12:86–102, especially p. 92. See also note 33 to follow.

24. Dewey does not discuss obligation in these lectures. See his discussion of moral good and obligation in the 1900 "Lectures on the Logic of Ethics," *LE*, pp. 52–54, 80–87, and the brief discussion in the "Lectures on Political Ethics" in this volume, chapter 13.

25. The crucial importance of resistance or opposition in moral inquiry is worked out in §77–80. See also the discussion of progress in the final section of the editor's introduction to the "Lectures on Political Ethics" in this volume.

26. *EW*, 4:259.

27. There is a brief discussion of the subject and predicate in judgments, without reference to the copula, in Dewey's 1900 "Lectures on the Logic of Ethics," *LE*, pp. 45–46.

28. For a similar statement, see the edited transcript of Steven Alan Nofsinger's *Dewey's Lectures in the Theory of Logic* (Ph.D. diss., Michigan State University, 1989). "Logic, instrumental logic, will furnish the key to the ultimate metaphysics or philosophy (which in this case will be ethical)" (129). In his "Logical Conditions of a Scientific Treatment of Morality," Dewey states that the "activity of judging does not exist in general," but "require[s] reference to an initial point of departure and to a terminal fulfillment." More particularly, "there must be something outside the most complete and correct collection

of intellectual propositions which induces to engage in the occupation of judging rather than in some other active pursuit." What is this "something outside"? "Only the whole scheme of conduct as focusing on the interests of an individual can afford that determining stimulus" (*MW*, 3:18).

29. Dewey, "An Analysis of Reflective Thought" (1922), *MW*, 13:61.

30. This conclusion appears to be the result of the "psychologist's fallacy" or "the reading into the early stages of a development that which can only be true of the latter stages, and can only be true of them just because it was not true of the earlier stages." See Dewey's 1898 "Lectures on Psychological Ethics," *LPPE*, p. 25. In chapter 1 of the first printing of *Experience and Nature*, Dewey refers to the tendency "to take the outcome of reflection for something antecedent" (*LW*, 1:375). Later discussion in chapter 1 is in line with the standpoint of this paragraph.

> Our constant and inalienable concern is with good and bad, prosperity and failure, and hence with choice. We are constructed to think in terms of value, of bearing upon welfare. The ideal of welfare varies, but the influence of interest in it is pervasive and inescapable. In a vital, though not the conventional, sense all men think with a moral bias and concern, the "immoral man" as truly as the righteous man; wicked and just men being characterized by bents towards different kinds of things as good. Now this fact seems to me of great importance for philosophy; it indicates that in some sense all philosophy is a branch of morals. (389)

However, the reader should note that these remarks are deleted from the second printing.

31. For a similar statement, see Dewey's "Logical Conditions," *MW*, 3:21.

32. See below, p. 9.

33. For this account of distinctions, see *Logic*, *LW*, 12:509–10.

34. This account of the individual/environment distinction is not worked out in these lectures. For a full discussion, see the 1898 "Lectures on Political Ethics," *LPPE*, pp. 271–80, especially p. 279.

35. See Dewey's 1900 "Lectures on the Logic of Ethics," *LE*, pp. xxvi, 83–85.

36. Dewey, "Three Independent Factors in Morals" (1930), *LW*, 5:284. This view is also worked out in Herbert W. Schneider, "Moral Obligation," *Ethics*, 50 (October 1939): 45–56.

37. This view of moral control is worked out in Dewey's *Democracy and Education* (1916), chapter 3, *MW*, 9:28–45; and his *Experience and Education* (1938), chapter 4, *LW*, 13:31–38.

38. See Rockefeller, *John Dewey: Religious Faith and Democratic Humanism* (New York: Columbia University Press, 1991).

[Introduction]

1. This Quarter's work is preliminary to Ethics proper. We are to consider the relation of ethical science to other forms of scientific inquiry and inquire into the formulation of ethical concepts. What is the relation of the ethical view of the world to the physical view of the world? The typical quarrels of philosophy circle about that point. Can there be a science of ethics? The logic of ethics is an examination of the method and not of the methods of ethics. Instead of asking what an ethical ideal is, we ask what an ideal itself is. This is a logical and not an ethical inquiry. The same is true of the concept of good; also with the idea of law. Back of the ethical inquiry is the inquiry into the nature of judgment.

2. Such an inquiry will practically be made with reference to the problems uppermost in the human mind. That phase is in general the conflict between the categories of the natural sciences and the categories of the ethical and social sciences, as between physical causation and final or teleological causation. In the physical sciences a fact is placed in reference to its antecedents. In conduct we explain facts in reference to their results. The antithesis is thus: physical causation vs. teleological causation; necessity vs. freedom; fact vs. ideal element; is vs. ought.

3. While the problem is in general the nature of the judgment, the particular problem is to see how these antithetic factors are related in the judgment. Every man must assert the unity of human experience. When we have gotten methods that have worked so well in the physical and biological sciences, it is inevitable that they should be introduced in ethical and social phenomena. This idea was first introduced by Comte.[1] If we have a science, there must be unity. The scientific impetus is back of the attempt to include social and political phenomena within the sphere of the other phenomena or facts of experience. Some ideas (as freedom) seem to evaporate when this method is pursued with ethical phenomena. On the other hand, there has been an effort, as with Kant, to mark off this sphere in which the mechanical principles are not found—a sort of dualism.

4. The fact that conflict is between motives common to all men indicates that analysis is defective. Examination has not gone far enough back. We shall then

analyze judgment to point out where we find unity. The view which makes universal the categories of the physical sciences is one-sided. The categories which become more explicit in the human and moral sphere throw light on the physical sciences.

[An Analysis of Judgment]

[Chapter 1. How Are Subject and Predicate Connected by the Copula?]

5. The fact that the judgment has a sensation as the subject expresses the fact, the "is" side. The predicate side implies consciousness, idea. The copula is always ultimately an act which comprehends the fact and idea. It is the only complete reality which ever exists. The others are abstractions. The question on the logical side is, "What is the subject? What is the predicate? How can they be connected in the copula?"

6. Looking at the judgment from the side of the subject, the subject has been discriminated. From the side of the predicate, the predicate has been unified. For example, "This is an envelope." Everything in the universe is "this," but here is discrimination. The subject has been limited. The predicate has been unified and identified. "Envelope" in the abstract has been identified with the subject of the proposition. The predicate by itself simply represents an abstract relation. Without the subject one might intelligently know "table," but not "concrete table."

7. It is evident then that it is the office of the copula to discriminate the subject and identify the predicate.

Identification
◄----------
Subject to Predicate
----------►
Definition

Here is the difficulty. How can one and the same process unite and divide? Must not one be reduced to the other, or one prove real and the other unreal? The nature of the copula appears to be such as to reduce judgment to mere tautological proposition or else to render the judgment false. Water is H_2O. If we emphasize the side of identity, what is the use of making the judgment? [Why not] simply say the subject is the subject[?]

8. Doctrine of the quantification of the predicate. [We] must not say "All men are mortal," but "All men are some mortal," so that it can be turned around. But this is false, for it can be shown that some mortals are not men, and a particu-

lar number of men must be the subject. So we have to carry the process until the predicate is coextensive with the subject. These are Locke's "trifling propositions," or Kant's "analytic propositions."

9. Taking the other side of the judgment it is equivalent to Kant's synthetic judgment. The difficulty on this side of differentiation or synthesis is that the judgment perverts the subject. "Chalk is white" is mere tautology or else the subject is changed when white is added as a new element. All knowledge implies discrimination but all knowledge changes your subject-matter. The next act changes that, etc. How then [do we] get any knowledge? This is the proposition underlying all intellectual scepticism. Here logic checks common sense. Here are facts and all we have to do is to go on and know them. But the very process changes the facts.

10. Common sense supposes the transformation means separating the two sides of the judgment. This analysis side gives us the logic of rationalism on one side. Kant adopted the premises of the rationalistic school and carried it to tautology, which was the suicide of rationalism.

11. The process of emphasizing the side of definition gives the logic of the empirical school. If the process of the empirical school were simply adding on the predicate, the proposition would be logically impregnable. But the predicate reacts on the subject and changes it; and the logical outcome must be scepticism, as that of rationalism must be tautology. The act of thought has always been a stumbling block to the empiricist. The real world is changed by the process. If we say the copula either identifies or discriminates, we say that it makes judgment either tautology or else perverts it.

12. Another definition of judgment is that it is the act of subsumption, i.e., placing a certain object in a certain class of objects. If we examine this we see that it comes to the same thing. If we ask what the act of classification is, it is said that the mind has experienced a number of objects, abstracts certain qualities, and generalizes. Comparison, abstraction, generalization—this is but going in a circle. For you cannot classify without making a judgment. We have simple tautology. This theory takes for granted certain fixed things at the outset. Their acts after that can be only a manipulation. Before being able to say "This is an envelope," [we] must know that a certain object is an envelope, before forming the judgment of the class envelopes.

13. Both of these schools assume something fixed outside of the judgment itself. The empiricist assumes that you start with a certain number of definite objects. The subject is fixed. The process of judgment is simply adding to or taking from the subject. The process of judgment does not enter into the construction of the subject-matter. The rationalistic school holds that something

definite is given, the concept or predicate, and the process of judgment is simply the identification of this concept with the subject-matter. The theory of the rationalistic school has always held to certain *a priori* fundamental concepts in order to get any knowledge at all.

14. Although these schools are opposed logically they have something in common. They have both taken something for granted outside of and independent of the judgment, though they differ as to what is given. Criticism must begin with this common characteristic. The meaning of the copula is purely formal with either school. If the subject is given, the "is" simply comes in to refer it to the predicate; and so if we take the other side, the "is" only gives a formal reference of the thing given to the act of judgment—the copula can have no intrinsic value.

15. Why should "is" be more than a mere point of reference of one to the other? The copula gives the statement of being, asserts the reality, and should not be treated as a mere representation of an act of mental predication. If it is merely subjective it contradicts itself. The judgment implies the existence of an object, and if the being is simply in the mind of the person forming the judgment, the judgment is a contradiction.

References:
Lotze, *Logic*, pp. 81–89, and notes pp. 2–10.
Bradley, *Logic*, pp. 98–108, and pp. 12–20.
Mill, *Logic*, Bk. I, Chaps. 4, 5, 6.
Bosanquet, *Logic*, Chapter on nature of Judgment and p. 22.

16. From the side of the subject the copula differentiates. From the side of the predicate the latter is held down to the concrete subject by the copula. Common sense and science both hold that the copula is objective in import. The most obvious objection to the contrary theory is the existence of negative judgments, e.g., "There are no ghosts" (cf. Bradley). The question arises, can any negative judgment stand alone? Negative form implies a positive assertion. "The nature of reality is such that it excludes ghosts." A merely negative assertion would be impossible. We cannot assert nothingness. We must have a positive concept of ghosts or sea serpents to make a negative judgment about them. When we say that there are none we do not negate the concept, but make a positive statement of the nature of reality.

17. Theories which reduce judgment to the mere act of subsumption, classification, likewise reduce the copula to something merely subjective. [There is] no reality in [the] class but only in the individual. "Whales are mammals." Theories assume that these individuals are included in [an] artificial class and clas-

sification is subjunctive only. If this is the nature of classification the reasoning is in a circle. But, besides, the scientific classification is an addition to the subject. The classification is a judgment of the nature of the thing, and we think we have gotten nearer to the real nature of the thing when we have made it.

18. Effort to classify by modern science is simply an effort to get at the life history of the individual. Here is the real classification according to evolution. The copula then must have objective import if classification means anything. "This whale is a mammal." [The] subject-matter is a definite reality, something there which affects the sense. No, the nominalist has always pointed out, there is no such thing as mammal; there are only individual mammals. The predicate of every judgment is an abstraction and as such is unreal. It is also a quality. Qualities have no existence of themselves. The copula has an objective reference, but that which the copula asserts to be real is unreal. [There is] no such thing as mammal.

19. On the side of the subject the same difficulty appears. [The] whale is real. It meets us in perception. But when we examine the subject it is at the mercy of the same judgment. There was a time when "whale" was only "this". By a long series of investigations and judgments it has become real. By condensation of knowledge the whale is taken as given but is a concept, a former judgment, "This is a whale." The subject is always a union of previous predicates, abstractions. Then the function of the copula being to assert reality, both subject and predicate appear to be abstractions. One abstraction is asserted of the other.

20. There are two methods by which logicians have tried to go beyond this point, not necessarily exclusive of each other. First, the reality of which the predicate is asserted is not the subject-matter of the given proposition but a reality which lies behind. "The whale is a mammal." The subject is not the idea whale, but a reality which lies farther back which is qualified as the whale (See also Bradley, pp. 50–51). This makes judgment unknown and unknowable. If this is true how can we say that these qualities can be predicated of the subject? If the subject is really unknown, how can it be said that subject and predicate can be connected in the judgment? Do not take it as meaning that the two are connected somewhere in the universe, but with a definition and specific case.[2] The connection then is unknown and unknowable (cf. Bradley, pp. 12–14). Not two ideas predicated, but the idea predicated of reality, is Bradley's position.

21. The principle behind all ethics is that the act of judgment involves both reality and idea. And the difficulties arise out of asserted antithesis between realities and ideas. The problem then is as to what is the relation between reality and ideas.

22. Second, [there is] the reduction of simple to hypothetical judgments. This is adopted by Lotze and Bradley. "I have the toothache." The only way in which

the statement can be made true is by qualifying the "I," by stating the connection in order that the judgment may be true. Then it becomes an hypothetical judgment instead of absolute. Only the former is absolutely true. Given the conditions there will always be the toothache.

23. So also with Lotze's "dog drinks." This is true only under certain conditions. The content of a hypothetical judgment is a statement of connection between certain qualities or conditions. If M then N. Or, whenever M then N. Wherever you have certain nervous conditions, there you have a toothache. This is a truly synthetic judgment, not a tautology. The protasis is one thing, the apodosis is another thing. Yet a connection between them is stated. They do not state that one thing is another thing, which is a contradiction unless mere tautology.

24. This reduction of positive to categorical solves the problem only by supposing the reality which is the ultimate subject of the judgment. The existence of fact is, if not denied, at least suppressed. When a statement is made of the conditions under which you have the toothache, the existence of fact is not asserted and cannot be. "If anyone trespasses he will be punished." [There is] nothing in this statement to posit [the] existence of [a] person trespassing. Reduction thus gets rid of the difficulty by reducing the judgment to ideal[ity].

25. All scientific judgment is hypothetical judgment. "When you find certain conditions, there you have the force of gravity." The hypothetical judgment is then universal and every universal judgment is hypothetical. But the universal judgment, because hypothetical, is ideal and not a statement regarding fact or existence.

26. Stock examples of formal logic "All A is B" claim to be both categorical and universal. If taken in extension they must be qualified. "All men are mortal" cannot be stated until all men now living have died. It has not been proved of every individual, but is believed to be true because [it is] taken in intention instead of extension and is thus reduced to an hypothetical judgment. A complete induction is only empirically universal and not rationally so. [We] could not take a single further step in induction. The judgment should take purely quantitative form.

27. A true universal must be quantitative and this is hypothetical and ideal. This comes [close] to saying, reduce the judgment to all predicate, the predicate of an implied but unasserted subject. This same point in another form is made by Bradley (the subject is the predicate). He takes "subject is predicate" and finds it more narrow. As given it is too vague. When the subject is further scanned all emphasis is laid on the predicate and the subject is simply implied.

28. The hypothetical judgment must presuppose a reality within which this connection of qualities holds, and yet it cannot assert that reality. If you sever

all connection of hypothesis with fact, the hypothetical judgment becomes pure nonsense. "If man trespasses he will be punished." Here it is taken for granted that there is a sphere of reality within which the connection is supposed to be true. It is the same contradiction as when the subject of the judgment is made a reality behind the judgment instead of in it. Does the predicate really qualify the subject? If not actually qualified by the predicate or connection of conditions in the hypothetical judgment, then put the reality outside of the sphere of the judgment. The reality is unknown and unknowable.

29. The discussion may be summed up by saying that in any way of dealing with it the fact or existence is the subject of the judgment and the idea or meaning is the predicate of the judgment. Or, psychologically, presentation or percept is the subject and concept or idea is the predicate of the judgment.

[Chapter 2. The Problem with Empirical and Idealist Theories]

30. There is one theory of the nature of judgment which seeks to solve the difficulty by suppressing the predicate or ideal element, which holds that all you need to do is to exhaustively describe your sphere of existence or fact. Educationally this is found in extreme specialism, which simply collects all the data possible and rejects all hypotheses. Physically, this leads to some form of realism.

31. The logical defect in this is that it contradicts itself. Description cannot be carried on consistently without reducing these facts to conditions. Wherever you have such and such facts, there you have something else. Take observations of facts about weather. The connections between those facts is more of a fact than the facts themselves. They are kept facts only by connecting them with each other. As the data are connected they group themselves coherently. Facts of southwest wind and hot day in Chicago always hold together. Either all the facts [are] absolutely isolated and [there is] no basis for grouping them, or there is a limit to the field of observation—an ideal which the most extreme specialist posits. Other facts are left out of the catalog.

32. This is the process of the so-called empirical or inductive logicians. They hold that the reality is always particular, and the predicate a certain view of the subject-matter. The predicate is all there in the subject. The universal has no reality. The general objection to this is that, carried out, these particulars supposed to be real things are reduced to circumstances or conditions. The assumption of this is that of a certain number of isolated particulars. But as the science goes on, these data become reduced to circumstances in a somewhat comprehensive relationship. This contradiction occurs because the general cannot be regarded simply as an abstraction from the particulars. For the general is assumed at the outset in the process of selection or limitation. With reference to an hypothetical already posited, the data are collected as relevant, or else all the facts of the universe must be collected.

33. All the empirical logicians have to assume certain relations, *viz.*, sequence in time and coexistence in space. That assumption still leaves some relationship which lies outside the facts, even as particular facts. We cannot say that any stroke of the hammer comes after another without expressing a relationship. It is not a part of the existence of a fact to come after another fact. The contra-

diction becomes greater when the idea of uniformity of sequence or succession is brought in. A very definite universal is here used. (See Venn, *Empirical Logic,* pp. 64–72.)

34. Thus the empirical logicians are driven to a mere tautology, or an hypothetical judgment. The predicate cannot be gotten out of the subject. The uniformity has to be read with the facts; it can never be gotten from them. This is recognized in Spencer's *First Principles.* The postulates of science cannot be proved by science. The law has to be assumed in the proof. If you prove that the weight of the products of combustion are equal to the material before [combustion], you have to assume that the scale and weight have remained the same.

35. The theory which recognizes the place which the predicate has in knowledge began with Kant. Omitting his technicalities, he attempted to show that neither percept by itself nor concept by itself constitute the judgment. All judgment implies a synthesis which is not given in the percepts. [We] can perceive a straight line only as the perceiver constructs the line—which involves a continual mental reproduction, and a continual mental synthesis. When a percept is a judgment, there is involved with it a process of synthesis.

36. Descartes, Leibniz, Wolff, etc., held that real knowledge was found in concepts, that mathematical and metaphysical knowledge is held in pure concepts. It is not from the percepts of a triangle that mathematical propositions are formed. According to them the certainty in Geometry comes from the investigation of the concept 'triangularity'. Kant shows that mere analysis of concepts gives mere trifling propositions. The certainty of the proposition regarding the triangle comes not through the concept of triangularity but from the process of the construction of the triangle. So in metaphysics from the idea of effect you get only idea of cause. There must be a synthesis of concept with fact existing outside of idea.

37. What, then, is judgment? Kant says that it is a synthesis of percepts (or perceptual elements) in or through a concept. This is the starting point of modern Logic. The concept then is only a way of constructing a perceptual product, and does not exist in reality by itself. Triangles were first made from practical necessity, and the concept could only be formed after the triangles had been made and the process was reflected on. The process of logical science is to turn around and examine the methods which had previously been unconsciously employed.

38. Kant holds that the great mass of concepts are extracted from percepts, so if we go far back enough we find that they are all derived from percepts. If the explicit predicate is empirical there is an implied concept which cannot be derived from percept. Imply concept of thing or quality. The concept of a thing

cannot be derived from the experience of a large number of things, because you cannot have a concept of a thing except as multiple sensations are reconstructed into a definite thing by the mind. Even sensations coming at the same time do not constitute a unity. There must be a basis for discriminating the coexistence of sensations. A category is, then, such a predicate as is necessary to constitute any subject-matter into subjects of intelligible judgments.

39. He carries analysis further. These fundamental predicates, being functions of unity, presuppose a unity, not only particular unification, but they imply the general idea of unity. There is some one unity in all these particular forms of unity. That is thought itself, the transcendental self or unity. The ultimate predicate of all judgment is the unity of thought or [the] unity of self (not a person but a function).

40. But the very explicitness of the analysis only makes the problem more peculiar. Union of both elements is necessary to make knowledge. How can they be united? What is this something which exists before knowledge? How can copula assert identity of things so heterogeneous? Kant shows that percept and concept have no value except as they are united in judgment, yet he gives them existence outside of the judgment. This is the fundamental difficulty in Kant's system. It has no unity between the act of predication in general and the particular act of predication. This unity of predication must be purely formal, and therefore is unrealizable in experience, because it is the process of connecting elements which are presented to thought. There is always more thought which has never been synthesized. This is simply saying that the concept, when disconnected, becomes hypothetical.

41. Another failure is found when we try to account for minor unities, e.g., gravitation or evolution. Kant attempts no solution in *The Critique of Pure Reason*. It cannot come from the side of sensation nor from the side of fundamental categories, for they are only formal. How can formal quantitative relation present itself in this particular quantitative relation? Having two presupposed independent elements, he can get no organic unity, nor can he get a particular unity.

42. Why [do] qualities of size, color, etc., of the table operate, instead of cause and effect? There must be some clue to sensation. If so, there must be some closer union between percept and concept than Kant permits. The work of logicians since Kant has been the effort to get rid of the hard and fast line at the bottom of Kant's dualism, to get rid of the formal empty character of the act of predication. (See Green, *Prolegomena to Ethics, Works*, Vol. II, pp. 184–94; Caird, *The Critical Philosophy of Kant*; Caird, "Metaphysics" in *Encyclopedia Britannica*; Royce, *The Religious Aspect of Philosophy*, Chap. 11.)

43. Green attempts to show that there is no judgment whatever without relations. Sensations can not give a relation. Relation is an act of thought. Coherence of experience demands an inclusive single system of relation, and implies the existence of an eternal, all comprehending thought. He attempts to
substitute for the empty unity of Kant a system of relations. Instead of being the
act of predication it is the whole system of predication.

44. Green still holds that for our knowledge the workings of this system of relations are dependent upon feeling. In the absolute this feeling could be reduced
to thought. In our experience this element of feeling can never be reduced to
thought. The result is that we know that there is such a system of relations, but
we cannot tell what it is. We can think and speak of it only in negatives. We cannot tell what it is positively because our experience is all under limitation. Feeling and thought must be one, and generally Green says that that one must be
thought, but we cannot tell what thought is. But Green starts out to deal with
the unity of our judgments and ends by denying that with which he starts out;
and finds real synthesis only in this system of relations which, after all, is simply an abstraction.

45. Caird's solution is much less formal than Green's. He holds that the perception and the conception are not essentially opposed to each other, as Kant
holds, nor permanently opposed to each other in our experience, as Green
holds. They are temporarily opposed to each other in our experience, but they
have a common source and are two phases of one unity. Both sensations and the
process of thought are evolved from a common substratum of feeling; and both
meet in the self which manifests itself, one side in multiplicity of sensations, and
on the other in unity of thought. There is no essential contradiction in Caird's
view, but his analysis is incomplete. Why does this unity of feeling break up into
those two elements? Or why and how does unity of self first divide itself into
two, and then bring those two together? The differentiation occurs on account
of judgment. But why does it thus break up and then reunite?

Feeling

Sensation   Conception

Unity of Self

46. Green tries to show the necessity of an all-inclusive system of relations.
No thought is true of itself; its truth consists in being in the right place in that
system. Royce gets at the same thing from the analysis of error. Each error implies a thought which includes the truth, and an infinite number of errors im-

plies an infinite truth. The fact of error implies another judgment which includes the truth. The same general criticism may be passed upon this as was passed upon Green.

47. To summarize: All judgment involves a fact or existence taken as the subject of the judgment qualified by the meaning or idea as predicate. The copula asserts objective unity of these two factors while the two factors themselves seem to be mutually exclusive.

48. Out of this apparent opposition logical schools have followed two opposite directions. One attempts to resolve the factor of existence into a system of concepts or relations. The other regards the concept as a mere abstraction from the fact, for mental convenience only. This latter tendency fails because this element of meaning, [which is] supposed to be abstracted from the fact, is necessary to constitute the fact. The former fails because it always has to set up a fixed datum of existence (experience), which is resolved into meaning or ideas, into relations. These two schools are those of the empiricist and idealistic logicians.

49. From a different point of view the idealist school can never show how the unity of thought is differentiated into variety. The unity of thought tends to remain purely formal, a bare principle of tautology. The empiricists are unable to account for the principle of identity, of unity involved in experience as a whole and every particular experience. If every judgment involves a union of these two elements, opposition must result from taking either element by itself.

[Chapter 3. The Significance of Tension and the Coordinating Function of the Copula]

50. There are two ways of going at the problem. One is to simply take it and try to solve it. This never gives satisfactory results in philosophy. The fact that it is a problem shows a contradiction and it can only be solved by supposing some [new?][3] element. The point is to get back of the problem and find the source of it. The problem then disappears. Here as everywhere the question is, how does this problem arise?

51. We have isolated the intellectual judgment from its place in experience as a whole. It has been isolated both on the side of its origin and on the side of its purpose. We have not asked what it evolves from nor what its function, purpose, is. The judgment is the logical unit, but this logical unit has itself only historical, not essential, unity. That is, it has the unity of being a certain phase of the development of conscious experience, but has no absolute unity. The problem has arisen because we have taken the historical unity as an absolutely inherent totality. It is like studying a bridge without taking into consideration the banks upon which it rests. The bridge in the air would be a contradiction.

52. The judgment represents the phases of the evaluation of experience. It is the process by which one value is changed for another value. Its meaning is not complete in itself, but is found in the value to which it leads up.

53. Neither does the judgment originate of itself from strictly logical considerations, but from the defect or break-down of some previous value. "Caesar crosses the Rubicon." The real significance of this is found neither in the subject nor predicate, but in the total idea of Caesar who made the advance to destroy the old decaying Republic. We get the complete image, the value of what results, in your mind.[4] "Mill wrote a Logic." If you did not know this before, you either enlarge Mill or Logic in your mind, according as [to how] you place emphasis. If [you are] studying logic, the value of Logic is enlarged.

54. The significance of judgment is in the process of judgment, not in its completion. When judgment is completed there is no judgment, but a certain value. As long as we are making out the judgment or familiarizing ourselves with it, the two elements of subject and predicate stand out as separate, but afterwards the value is a single idea in the mind. This value is the true copula, e.g., a new element in the air, [a] theory of evolution. A new larger fact is substituted for the old subject and predicate of the judgment.

55. What is this value which is thus substituted for the old value? Is the value simply a subject or predicate for further judgments? That is one meaning of the new value.

56. Is that the only value judgment has? If we have only a new and larger subject or predicate for the judgment, what is the result? If judgment has intrinsic value, what is the nature of this inherent worth? How are we to express it? Symbolization is the setting before the mind of the method of getting an experience of the judgment. Realization is the actual concrete experience. The contradiction which the rationalist and idealist fall into is caused by the failure to see that judgment is not completed until realized. The realization is the copula which has absorbed into itself both subject and predicate.

57. A lot of scientific formulae are but predicates. A judgment has two typical stages of development: one of symbols, of methods; the other the carrying out of method, the realization. Until there is the realization there is a contradiction. What is the force in education except the attempt to substitute a vital personal experiencing for a more scholastic abstract? The movement of science itself, the fact that it is experimental, and the whole logic of the process of unification, are based upon this. In unification we construct a new experience, the way to which has been pointed out by the hypothesis, and which must be a realization.

58. From this standpoint, what is the significance of subject, predicate, and copula? For example, "Sugar is sweet." Carried back to the stage of symbolization, what does the fact side stand for? What does the idea stand for? What does a noun stand for? What an adjective? Water is H_2O. To a chemist discovering it or a person rediscovering it, what is water? Not an ultimate fact, but material to be taken into a certain action. H_2O is an hypothesis to be realized, the end to be reached, the method or way to act, to work.

Subject	Predicate
Material	Way
Conditions	Method

The percept is never the complete reality, but is simply setting before the mind certain material to be used. The concept is the way of grasping the material. The copula is the complete reality. The judgment may give new fact (realization) or it may give new truth to modify other things (symbolization). The predicate is not a form, is not static in the sense of a skeleton or mold, but is active like an architect's plan. It is dynamic as opposed to static.

59. If the above is true we see how the fundamental contradiction which we have been dealing with disappears. Strict logicians have said, "The fact is one sort of thing and the idea is some other sort of thing. How [do we] get these two things, so unlike as existence and form, together?" One school [the empirical] tried to obviate the difficulty by assuming fact as the connection. The difficulty with this is that we cannot eliminate all the ideal element[s] from the fact. This is the difficulty when the judgment is isolated and resolved into fact. The idealistic school, which resolves judgment into thought, has to assume a certain basis of fact which gives the starting point for concepts. At least as far as our own existence is concerned, there must be a substratum of percepts from which concepts can be derived.

60. The present standpoint which we have reached solves the problem by dissolving it. It comes to the [following] formula: The nature of action is such as to distinguish itself into means of action on the one side and method of action on the other. The action is ultimate and has for its law the differentiation of itself and realizing itself in idea. What we call fact or existence is simply something to operate with and has no objective validity itself. It is not rigid; it changes as we develop as individuals and as a race. Both fact and idea then change all the time according to the quality of action or interest (in psychological terms).

61. From this point we develop it along psychological lines. Take "Sugar is sweet." First, what is seen, say color, is the primary datum. Is color an activity or is it objective? The former is from the psychological standpoint. It is a datum, not simply as quality, as perceived, or as object, but as the activity of the mind. Color represents a mind activity and it does not exist objectively. To avoid mistakes we will say that the primary datum is "act of seeing." So we have:

stimulus - - - organic reaction

color - - - act of seeing

It is act of seeing only when we have [an] object and organ. This datum is immediate, but we have mediate data, the memory of touching, smelling, tasting, etc. These last are not wholly ideal, for in memory there is incipient starting of immediate centers. But in so far as they are ideal they are predicates. To get the real predicate, the interest must arouse some special element which is, here, tasting.

62. But these are simply implicit, undeveloped judgments. When does the judgment become explicit or actual? We cannot get the explicit judgment until we in some way compare these two data, the immediate and the mediate. Otherwise there will be simply substitution of one act for another. There must be

resistance. How does experience "sweet sugar" get translated into this other idea "Sugar is sweet"? The primary experience is a somewhat mediate experience, for act of seeing is [a] more primary activity (vision, touching, tasting). If without any tension or opposition the seeing could at once pass over to tasting, we would have a substitution of one experience for another and there would be no experience which would take the form of a judgment.

63. What would occur if there were some opposition? How does the concept come into the mind at all? What sets the mind to comparing, to abstraction? How does abstraction ever occur? Suppose an object is out of reach. The visual activity is overflowing into the touch and taste centers. The mouth waters even though the sugar has not been tasted. Then either attention might be distracted, or the substitution of one experience for another [would occur], and these activities would die out of consciousness.

64. But if a child should refuse to allow either of these? Through this resistance the subject and predicate are set off from each other. The stimuli are going on all the time; yet activities do not complete themselves and there is a return wave. There is an impulse to complete experience by touching what we have seen. The result is that the immediate side is set off as actual but nonsatisfactory. There is no doubt about the seeing, and the satisfactory sweetness is nonactual as far as the image is striving to realize itself. Then the image of sweetness is more or less marked off distinctly from the seeing, and the more this thwarting goes on the more distinct is the idea. It is there as a means of setting up the other activity. By the repetition of such experience[s], sugar as an object of vision is marked off from sugar as sweet substance; getting the sweetness is necessary to complete the sugar.

65. Fact and idea, percept and concept, are not given existences. The distinction between them is functional, a distinction of the place which each occupies in the whole experience. It is a radical error to distinguish them as actual, as distinctions in reality itself. Fact of existence is that phase of activity which is immediate or initial, but which does not satisfy on its own account, [and] which is not complete as immediate, but whose existence is reduced to a means of stimulating another phase of activity, of experience, imaged as satisfactory or necessary to complete the first. The idea, or percept which becomes the concept, is the mediating phase of an activity stimulated by the primary and necessary to give it unity or completeness.

66. The empirical school contends that the concept is a convenience, not a reality, not an absolute thing. But the fact as fact is just as much convenience, is no more reality itself than is the concept. It is not a merely mental or subjective convenience. It is a convenience in that it has a function in experience as

such. The idealistic school has to postulate a sense element from which thought starts and against which it works, because the thought or meaning is always mediate. Its very nature is mediation. It is a process of valuation, and therefore postulates the material to be valued. These distinctions of subject and predicate are induced within the growth of an activity.

67. As a functional distinction, the subject stands as stimulus and provides the means or conditions. If the child is to get the experience of [the] sweetness of sugar it must have stimulus, whether the sugar is seen or merely suggested. The process of association will go back somewhere to where something was present.

68. The predicate serves as end to be reached by means. It is the goal which fixes the channel in which the immediate activity will discharge. The visual center has a large number of motor connections. Along which of these will the mental activity discharge? Will it end in touch, taste, running away, etc.? It will discharge along the path of least resistance, but the excitation at the other end determines what the path of least resistance is. This, under normal conditions, and unless there is a breakdown in the psychological machinery. The goal is not absolute, but defines the limits of activity. [Hitting the] target is not the game, any more than arrows are the game, but only [a] means of valuation.

69. A few points on the psychological side. First, suppose we adopt the habit theory. Its weakness is in supposing a habit results from sheer repetition. One successful coordination will set up the habit for all time, but many unsuccessful ones will not set up the habit. A child learning to walk repeats wrong movements many times, but only when it hits upon the right ones does it set up a habit. The principle of habit cannot be understood except with reference to an end. There are certain lines of least resistance, but these come to be such in performance of a function or reaching an end. This particular path becomes one of least resistance because it is the most successful.

70. Second, the relation between the sense and the brain. Functionally the relation of sense organs and brain ought to parallel the relation between subject and predicate. The predicate would stand for the motor tendencies, the discharges which are just starting out. We cannot see a piece of chalk after becoming familiar with it without having a tendency to pick it up and write with it, or to crumble it, etc. Hypnotism illustrates the principle more completely, where every suggestion is isolated and at once acted upon. This doctrine began perhaps in Bain's "primitive credulity." Baldwin's later work on dynamogenesis carries this out. Fouillée bases his whole philosophy on the idea itself as force.

71. Third, there are three [phases in forming a judgment]: (1) the previous

coordination, corresponding to the subject-matter of the judgment, (2) the shooting around of these in the brain constitutes the copula, the efforts at coordination, (3) the nascent discharge is the predicate. The whole judgment (when the copula is not merely formal) is swallowed up in the copula. It is the tension between the sense organs and the motor discharge and muscles, or whatever corresponds to the sense organs. The brain represents the tension between two acts, one on the subject side, the other on the predicate side. Without a brain we would be a prey to all the stimuli that acted upon us. Without the center the strongest stimuli would prevail and there would be pulling and hauling on all sides. The copula, the act of coordinating, may, in analysis, be set over against the thing to be coordinated. The coordination is the completed thing, when the act of coordination passes over into it. As long as the child is able to eat sugar whenever it wants it, while sugar is a physically distinct object, it [sugar] is not psychically distinct. Only as the tension between the various predicates arises do the objects themselves become distinct. If everything it sees is to be put in the mouth, sugar does not exist for it as a distinct thing.

72. It is an error to assume that because we now have the discriminated things we have always had them. Judgment, in the outcome, arises from means (subject) and direction (predicate). [The] copula becomes [the] tension between habit and aim. It originates from resistance in the activity. Judgment is the transitional stage between one unified activity and another unified activity.

73. The common error of intellectual and empirical schools is that they isolate the judgment. The logical process is what we call the intellect. It is the process of mediating the activity, of developing value in activity. The logical is the intermediary between the psychological and the ethical. Logic cannot be isolated from psychology. It is the derivative side. Neither can we discuss the logical, the intellectual, apart from its aim or function, the ethical.

Unified Activity

Psychological	Derivation
Habit	Aim

Logical Judgment

Means	Direction
Ethical	Aim, Function

Unified Activity

What does this mediation do? On the side of origin the judgment arises through tension. [There are] two results, according to the way this tension is taken. Is the resistance in the activity or to the activity? Activity needs stimulus and that stimulus implies resistance. This resistance is encountered by running into something outside of self, or the activity develops within itself the two factors of resistance and the force to overcome resistance, stimulus and response.

74. Illustration of the first theory is found in the relation between the systems of Kant and Fichte. Kant has a dualism which he could not unify. Fichte started out with the assumption that there must be a unity. The "I" cannot realize itself without some stimulus, but Fichte held that that stimulus could not be outside of the self. The problem for Fichte was to find some common trunk from which the sense and reason might arise. There is no meaning in pure light unless there is something for it to break against. The world would be just as much a blank with pure light as with pure darkness. The eye cannot see light. So there must be a limit to the self to realize itself at all. There is no self-consciousness except the self [to] be limited, yet the self cannot be limited by anything material.

75. Fichte's position was that the ego simply posited the world of sense. The ego reflects itself into a non-ego by unconscious means. This limit being set up, the pure self realizes itself against it. This is only a restatement of the problem. It does not solve it. Hence it is a begging of the question. Suppose the pure self succeeded in the work of realizing itself. That realization would be a failure. It would return to a condition of *quietus* again. The self first makes believe it has this limit. Then it tries to get rid of this limit. If it succeeds it would be worse off than before.

76. Fichte's position shows where this dualism leads to. But he holds all the time that the sense is subordinate to reason, even that it is negative and valuable only as a stimulus. But the contradiction is that when you get this pure reason there is no value in it because [it is] without discrimination. Thus he has not really overcome the dualism in the Kantian standpoint. Functionally, he has to. The function of experience is to eliminate sense. Reason, ego, is considered as a goal to be reached, not as an organ by which to progress.

77. Here is the question which underlies all schools of philosophy; this ever present dualism. The various views reduce themselves to this. According to one the sense material is regarded as resistance to self, the function of experience being to minimize, eliminate, or assimilate sense, while self is looked upon as a goal to be reached. According to the other view the distinction between sense and reason, between subject and object, is evolved; and within the process of experience, the production of this distinction is positive and valid. And [in] the distinction being evolved, sense plays the part of means or condition, and rea-

son the part of a plan or instrument or direction of action in realizing another unified experience. That is, sense is not something to be overcome but to be produced. Reason or thought, instead of being the goal, is a plan or method of reaching. Reality reached by the logical process is this process of distinguishing subject and predicate, and of re-uniting them into a single total value.

78. Goals are just as much local and temporary as standpoints. The concept of 'goal' is also relative, or historical, as well as [a] standing point. The reality is the whole process, the activity which continually produces discrimination and leads on to unified experience again. (See diagram above.) Why we get this relative fixity we will consider later on. Not only are goals temporary, but the concept 'goal' is also temporary. There is no absolute goal. We constantly create the goal. So, not only are the inner goals relative, but the goal "perfection" is also. We continually set up a new goal or end, not because of the failure of a previous one, but because of the success in reaching past goals.

79. The question is whether resistance is with[in] the activity or to it. The goal being objectivity, the resistance would be without. But the goal being as above indicated, the resistance would be within. If we identify ourselves with one part of the organism all resistance would be without and to it, e.g., [we] would suppose the skeleton existed first, and the extensor and reflexor muscles added, instead of being all developed together. Unless there is a comprehensive whole there can be no question of resistance. The concept of resistance involves the idea of a system or totality within which that resistance occurs. If the resisting and resister were independent they could never get near enough, get the relations to each other, that resistance demands.

80. Suppose you are prying up a stone with a lever and the stone resists the lever. Why does it resist and therefore stimulate greater effort put in[to] the lever? It is not the fact that it exists, but the fact that it exists as resistance to consciousness. Mechanically, resistance grows out of a redistribution of motion. As another illustration, take a conflict of organs within the organism, say between the eye and touch. A child when it sees a beautiful thing wants to look at it; it also wants to play with it and break it up. There is a conflict between different organs. But the only reason that the conflict can take place is that both are organs of the same organism. If they were in different organisms, no conflict could take place. Not only must [both] be physically present, but because [they are present,] each, eye and hand, represents the whole organism from its standpoint.

81. The eye is not only distinct from the hand; in evolution it has taken into its activities the result of previous activities of the hand, e.g., it affirms that the table is smooth from just looking at it. It is not so easy to illustrate from the history of the race, but processes must go on just the same. Why should there be distinctions of color, say between red and green, unless green stands for some-

thing to eat and red for something to run away from? An iron-worker sees many shades of red, where we see but one, because each one means something to do, to him. The whole psychology of discrimination reduces itself to this.

82. The other phase of the question is the meaning of it. What is the function of this tension? Evidently the answer of this is conditional upon the result just reached. It makes all the difference whether it is within or to the activity. If it is to the activity, the significance of the resistance must be negative. It exists simply to be overcome or reduced. It is a necessary evil. If it arises within, there is a presumption that this tension has an organic significance, that it has a value in the activity itself. That organic significance is found in the fact that this tension is the law of growth for evolution. It is the process of bringing to consciousness or realizing value in the tension or resistance. Certain values are made to stand out distinctly from each other before consciousness; and after the tension is resolved and we have a unified situation, or completed experience, this experience has more significance and value than the one out of which it arose prior to the tension.

83. As a psychological illustration take the process of learning to play on the piano. Before learning, the auditory and motor sensations will be more or less fused, especially with a person of average musical ear. The process of learning is the process of causing certain sensations to stand forth by themselves out of the sensory continuum. The difficulty in learning is found in causing those sensations to stand out and in coordinating them with each other. The learning is the process of bringing out these tensions. The coordination marks the copula. When the coordination is completed, the person has learned to play and has one completed experience.[5] Those other activities have no longer a distinct place in consciousness, except when it is necessary to learn a new and difficult piece. The new experience is just as much a unified state as the one from which it arose, but is of much greater value.

84. The outcome contains that process of resistance absolved. This is difficult to state. It is one thing to mark a vital experience and another to make a definite statement about it. The moment we attempt to define it we go back to the standpoint of existence or mediation.

85. The best way is simply to illustrate it so that we can realize it in our own consciousness. The outcome of the process of learning to walk is the automatic walking. In one sense that activity has become unconscious. But that is only when we isolate the mechanical side of walking. The activity of walking is at the same time the focus of the child's various sensations. All are related to it and subordinated to it. When walking is automatic, the reaction of this value of locomotion into sensation takes place. Visual and other activities are now set free.

The eye experiences have now indefinite extensibility as we walk around. The eye before was limited to the particular set of stimuli which affected it in a particular location. The eye also takes into itself at the present moment greater depth and content of meaning, which in a practical sense may be termed intuitional, e.g., extension, etc. These have been brought to it through walking and other muscular activity. As a focus, walking has lapsed into unconsciousness, but the value of it is broadened and intensified in consciousness. (See James' psychological fallacy.[6])

86. In everyday experience this process of mediation has dropped out as soon as possible, e.g., the difference between reading a book and proof reading. Persons are often blind in one eye for a long time without knowing it. When in the scientific position, the whole interest is in getting at the history rather than at the outcome in analyzing these processes of mediation. This process is the real reality, and the outcome is more or less of an illusion. The syncretic[7] experience of color is resolved into vibrations of the ether on the one hand and the nervous structure of the eye on the other. These distinctions then go back into the qualitative consciousness. This latter cannot be stated objectively, but must be experienced.

87. To complete a scientific process, the conditions have to be set up, and the experience realized. The fallacy is in identifying science with the process of analysis. The scientific reality is the completed experience. The scientific process as expressed in the middle stage is the statement of a method of getting a certain experience: the criticism of experience. [It] tells how to get the experience of color so that you not only will have it but will know how to get it and what you have gotten. This is all that can be put in books. It is a complete account of the way to get an experience, but it is not the experience. This is the significance, logically, of any judgment. No intellectual conception of this university is the university, but the record of past and the announcement of future work give the University greater value. This last stage is the one of highest self-consciousness. When the attention is absorbed by the process—the tension, the method—there is not the highest self-consciousness, e.g., [a] person engaged in religious or benevolent activities is most highly self-conscious, though if absorbed in the reasons for so acting he is less so.

[Chapter 4. Intellectual, Aesthetic, and Moral Value][8]

88. The next step is to attempt to classify the various types of value which this qualitative realization assumes: the logical or intellectual, the aesthetical, and the moral.

89. The previous account is in a way incomplete. While the logical process has to be treated as a process of mediation, the intellectual process, to the person pursuing it, becomes an end in itself. The process of learning appeals to us on its own account. But this learning also is experience. It is a process of mediation and yet it is itself immediate. The intellectual interest is essentially an interest in the fact of the tension. It implies the setting and the solving of a problem. Apart from problems there is no intellectual interest. Curiosity, wonder, scientific method all imply this problem. This shows but positive meaning and limitation of its meaning. The tension must be developed to have any consciousness. It is an interest in the fact and form of tension, rather than its content.

90. The intellectual interest is in the copula as formal, in the factors independent of their relation and union. This means that the development of self is not here deep enough for the implication of the self in the material to be recognized. The self is that which operates on the material, but the facts which are operated upon are not seen to have any organic relation to the self. That means again that the tension is not felt to be in and of the self in its deepest sense. The tension is given to the self, and all mind has to do is to find out the tension and state it properly. It is not realized that the tension is actually the outcome of the self, the doings of the self. Unless we do know where the tension is, successive activity cannot be full. It is more or less blind and tentative, [and] is working without a knowledge of the facts to be unified. When interest goes beyond the interest to find and state what the tension is, then the interest becomes aesthetic.

91. It seems sometimes that a contradiction is stated when it is said that the intellectual process is one of mediation, and yet has a value in itself. It is the purpose which is mediate. It is a fact of itself, and thus has a value in itself; and there is no contradiction in saying that it is preparatory to something else. The truer it is at the time, the more is its value in the function to be used. A person making a watch, if thinking too much about the purpose, will not do his work best. Yet this thought of the purpose gives the criterion for the correctness of the parts and their adjustment with each other. A person interested in a scientific pursuit must be interested in the investigation for its own sake. If he is too much concerned with the question of its possible good or evil outcome, he will be dis-

qualified for the scientific investigation. But the more the outcome is realized the deeper will be the intellectual interest. The intellectual interest is in an abstraction, but the function of the abstraction is to lead up to the concrete whole. It is an error to try to make the process come out at a predetermined end, as was done in the middle ages.

92. On the ethical side the two abstractions appear again. The intellectual interest is the proper sphere of the tension. The ethical interest is in arresting the tension—the intellectual interest—at a certain point and turning it to some practical end. The more a person's intellectual interest is developed, the more adequate is his treatment of the tension, e.g., the man who sees conflict between capital and labor in relation to their development finds intellectual but not moral antagonism.[9]

93. The moral antagonism is the setting up of one thing against another in action. This is the intellectual distinction arrested. It is not true that society will be better without antagonism or tension, but that tension is in its proper moral place in the intellectual sphere, i.e., as furnishing the conditions of action but not the principles of action. If the antagonism is accepted as a fixed fact, the development is distorted. The intellectual antagonism furnishes more things to unify.

94. Aesthetic Value. These three values are not three things. They are simply names which we give to one process according to the stage at which we take it. Analytically the stages may be marked off; the very nature of the process is not to stop but to go right on. The interest becomes aesthetic when the copula absorbs the subject and the predicate into itself instead of simply relating activity between them, or when the tension and the solution of the tension are both felt within the self's own experience. Interest is not now in the fact of tension but in the self as comprehending or containing the tension. Self here means total experience. The problem interest becomes the plot interest. It is a problem when the antithesis is most prominent. It passes into a plot when we see the unity which includes the elements of the problem, and is developed and maintained by these elements. As soon as we get a unity in the evolution of the intellectual interest which is not incompatible with the tension, we have an aesthetic interest.

95. Scientific interest in a landscape would be geological and botanical. The aesthetic interest is the unity, the adaptation of vegetable life to its environment, etc., the concentration of the process of evolution in this living whole. This is a deeper aesthetic interest than the unconscious appreciation of the tension, conflict, evolution, which the casual observer has for the landscape. (Cf. Royce, *The Spirit of Modern Philosophy*, p. x, ff.)

96. Aesthetic experience marks the realization of the self-unity as that has been mediated through a process of conflict. The consciousness of the struggle is lost, in one sense, in the outcome, the unity.

97. Probably every period that marks a deeper appreciation of nature follows a period of contrast. The appreciation of the beautiful would follow the consciousness of the hostile world. This appreciation, however, has been worked out throughout the experience of the whole race, e.g., the color green must be the outcome of some past process of coordination. From this point of view it is obvious that the transition from the aesthetic to the intellectual is necessary. If there is any synthesis objectively there, the process of analysis must reveal it, and the synthesis will not be in opposition to the analysis.

98. All the great scientific discoveries have been the result of definition. As soon as the mathematical analysis is completed the unity is seen. The scientific process is in unstable equilibrium. It always tends to reveal a unity which, when appreciated, gives us a deeper aesthetic view.

99. From the standpoint of logic any essential permanent opposition between science and poetry is impossible. The aesthetic experience is distinct from the intellectual, but the latter must bring out the unity. It does not follow that this will be true of any individual, but the outcome must sometime be realized in some individual. The intellectual experience carries within itself a movement which will carry it beyond itself.

100. How with the aesthetic experience? Is not the logical stopping of it there? The answer must be "No!" because the contemplative appreciation of a unity always stimulates motor organs. It tends to new production. In aesthetic language the function of works of art as contemplated is (must be) always educative. The eye cannot rest in a certain landscape as seen, but is trained in a certain habit of seeing. And the habit must go beyond the things seen. So also with hearing music. A child cannot be surrounded with ugly things without forming the habit of seeing things in that way, and then of doing ugly things. The historical education of the Greeks to sculpture, of the Italians to painting, of the Germans to music, arises from habits formed.

101. The contemplation cannot end in itself. The perceiving side immediately passes over into the active. Emerson's essays on art work this out better than any other writings. The work of art tends to produce the artistic habit. The aesthetic culminates in the work of art. Hence the futility of producing a class of artists by themselves. Only when the people have the artistic habit can the artist be produced. The average artist will not see beauty in the landscape before other people see it in business, etc. Technical training may be had when the aesthetic experience has been developed; and the great artist will help the people see it in

business, landscape, etc. By setting free the organs the aesthetic experience passes on the other experience.

102. A new tension of a different kind—not between objects as objects but between a thing and a standard, between a habit and a particular case—is now set up. This typical habit, once formed, becomes a standard for all particular habits. This marks the transition into conscious moral experience. This formula is historically verified. Conscious moral generalizations have arisen out of a background of artistic work. The moral standard by which all particular things are to be tested has been the outcome of such work.

103. We get standards from the Greeks. The parallelism between Confucius and Aristotle is to be accounted for by the artistic background. We do not get them from the Hebrews or Romans. The moral consciousness of the Hebrews was immediate, without the process of referring to a standard. In Rome the standards were objective, not intellectual. The standards were in institutions. Neither Hebrews nor Romans had the aesthetic ideals such as the Greeks had. It was the action of the Greek ideals upon the Romans which produced the Roman Law. There is no other way but art, *a priori*, by which that could have arisen. Mechanical and industrial processes could give it, but only when they became artistic, when they guide themselves by the general considerations of fitness and rhythm, where the processes are held down to the following of rules and precedents. The aesthetic consciousness did arise from manual machinery. The Greeks were good artists because they were good workmen. The great artist will rest upon the generalizations of technical workmen behind him.

104. The Moral Value. The limitation of the intellectual experience was that it was interested in the fact of the tension, the material being presupposed. The activity of dealing with them is referred to the mind, but the material is given. In the moral experience the material belongs to the self, just as much as the process of dealing with the material. The subject is the sense object. The predicate is the law or statement. Those are both, rather [than just the presupposed material,] to be given to the intellectual experience. In the moral experience the sense objects become our own appetites and impulses. The predicate is the law as regulative and normative. The self is in the subject and predicate just as much as in the copula. The eye from the moral point of view is an organ both controlled so as to give us certain results [and] which strives to work in certain ways or is directed to work in certain ways.

105. In the aesthetic experience the process of experience is assumed. We get the outcome. The moral experience has to realize that this process of struggle is the self. The struggle as a struggle always falls outside of the aesthetic experience. In the moral experience the working out of the process is consciously re-

alized. The aesthetic experience always transcends itself. In logical terms it gives no qualitative value as a something which can be completed in quality, in a moment. It gives us a world which has summed up its meaning as if it were over for all, or eternal. It gives us a cross-section of the process of experience. It is not presented to the self but the self is a present self, otherwise it could not be contemplated.

106. The existence of time has no meaning from the aesthetic point of view. This comes out historically in Plato and Aristotle. According to the latter, practical activity is finite. It implies that a person wants something which he lacks. It is then unworthy of God because it would imply that the Absolute is not perfect. God cannot then have purposes or ends. He is not passivity, but the activity is intellectual. He means here that the activity is contemplation and thus aesthetic. Platonic ideas are essentially of the aesthetic type. Thus the existence of the imperfection of the finite world becomes a problem, but one which cannot be solved.

107. The temptation, then, from the aesthetic point of view, is that it takes experience apart from the process from which it arose and apart from the process into which it passes. The aesthetic is the regnant idea in philosophy. The moral standpoint is that this tension is just as much the activity of the self as is the realization of a single value which is its outcome. The moral experience conditions both the intellectual and the aesthetic whether we take them from the side of the derivation or the side of direction. Sensation considered as appetite precedes sensation considered as discrimination or sensuous quality. The eye is primarily a motor organ and thus precedes the function of the eye which gives agreeable colors, etc. The sensations considered as intellectual or aesthetic are simply the objectification of the sensations considered as an organic impulse.

108. The question as to whether their[10] universals were before or after, or identified with the individual, was not metaphysical at first but ethical. Distinctions that afterwards became metaphysical or logical were at first ethical. How could the mind become conscious of law unless it had first become conscious of a universal principle? What constitutes qualities [as] "common" or how does the mind observe the common property? Or what is the motive for abstracting it [the common property] and setting it up as a principle? It is only because we act on them that we become conscious of their common properties. We cannot manage our own acts except as we recognize them as actions.

109. If we say law is a reality we are realists. If we say it is purely nominal and that the real universality is an arrangement of words, we are nominalists. These points of view fail to recognize that directive function which our experience gives us in attaining to another experience. The universal is not a reality and yet

every reality is a universal because it enters into the real direction of our experiences. From the nominalist point of view the word is not universal but has the practic[al],[11] regulating or directing quality.

110. If the moral conditions the intellectual on the side of origin as well as the outcome, it conditions the aesthetic the same way. That presentation has had a history. Thus realization of the unity is the solution of a problem and if we took away from the experience what it has it would lose its aesthetic quality. It leads on to motor reaction and its final significance is in the habits thus formed.

111. It does not follow that the aesthetic and intellectual experience must be abstracted and that the moral may not. It is not necessary that the former should be isolated. On the other hand, moral experience may be abstracted, though it is less abstract, and includes more than the others.

112. The phase of experience known as the religious is any one of the others taken adequately and not abstracted. It is not a fourth thing. It is any one of these realized adequately, taken as a phase of the whole, and therefore having the meaning of the whole taken back into it. Any experience which can demand the whole devotion of the being is religious. It is closer to one than to another.

113. In the above it has been attempted to give definitions of intellectual, aesthetic, and moral, and not to take them as ready made. They are not entities. Beauty, goodness, etc., are not things existing by themselves. These terms have been evolved as we have come to these various phases of experience. Attempts to define religion have been made in terms of the relationship between God and man, man and the unknowable, etc. Any activity which is capable of calling forth all these powers is a religious experience.

[Chapter 5. Reconciliation of Scientific and Moral Views of the World]

114. The problem which determines the special problems which writers take up is the possibility of reconciling the scientific view of the world with the moral view. Science seems to eliminate self. The scientific view seems to give us a world from which ends are excluded, from which freedom is excluded. Setting up a moral sphere seems to be an illusion which our own ignorance has made possible. This seems to have been the outcome of the scientific process.

115. On the other hand, the moral interests have been too great to put out of the way without a struggle. Hence we have philosophizing and the resulting dualism. This is found everywhere since Kant. Various attempts have been made, as above indicated, to deal with this dualism.

116. In Kant an attempt is made to fence off the two worlds, in one of which the moral categories have sway, in the other the scientific method. Evidently this is not a solution of the problem. The practical question is whether we must not give up the moral sphere or else set up a dualism as in Kant.

117. Another solution is implied in previous discussions. That is, in brief, this setting off of this world of objects and laws with which science deals over against moral experience, is itself a phase in the development of experience as practical or moral. The world of objects and sensations constitutes the defined activity. This is set off for a practical purpose. The process of definition is a process of securing the accurate and economical and efficient conditions and stimuli to activity. The world of objects is either an aesthetic world or a world of instruments to action. A tree, if attended to but for a moment, is an aesthetic object. If I go on to define it I am taking it as an instrument to give shade, make fire, promote a point of guidance for locomotion, etc.

118. The only attempted verification of these hypotheses, here, is that they give unity to our experience. It shows how the problems have arisen and how we may get rid of them.

119. A scientific justification of it would require, first, a biological verification, that is, showing that, historically, the sense organs, and hence the sense activities, have been developed and conserved on teleological grounds because they are practical servants in life. If this could be shown it would be proved that the world of objects is the objectification of experiences. The separation of objects from ourselves would cease. Second, the history of human culture in the widest sense, [serves] to show that the distinction between various objects and

the classification of objects serves the same practical end. The verifications cannot now be given.

120. The hypothesis means that objectivity is to be interpreted not as something lying over against psychical activity but as something thrown out with reference to psychical activity. Etymologically the word ['objectivity'] cannot be taken as something lying over against; [n]or 'activity' as something that is thrown [out] in the sense of having relation to [objectivity] and not [as existing] in the static sense. The reason why a world of objects is also a world over against activity is because of the principle of continuity or habit-in-action itself. We have produced these tools and now cannot get away from them. We must understand them before carrying the activity further. Future activity is conditioned by what has been done. Therefore the externality of the world is simply the reflex of this necessity. Future activity must be carried on through adjustment to the past.

121. The radical fallacy of all materialism, the attempt to generalize experience from this point of view, is that it takes as ends what are only means or instruments. Activity has done its work so thoroughly and completely that it has given these objects a certain relative independence of any particular purpose. They may be put to so many uses that it seems that they are not means for any purpose and are ends in themselves. Objectivity is the definition of activity. (See *The Psychological Review*, Nov. 1895, Baldwin on "The Origin of Things.") Materialism results from taking means for ends. Means have been so completely developed that they seem indifferent to ends as such. With the growth of the division of labor, of the intellectual interest *per se*, this tendency increases greatly. The scientific calling is not concerned with ends as such.

122. The history of theory and practice has still to be written. If written, it would carry out the statement that this abstraction of means from end is temporary. All scientific results tend to enter into life as a whole. Astronomical investigations seem to be remote from real life, yet they have simply revolutionized men's typical social and religious ideas. [Take, for example,] making the sun the center [of the solar system] and getting ideas of motion, and [then] the latter became a generic idea. Abstract mathematical and physical investigations condition industrial life of today. Many things may never have been put to practical use, but the method is reflected in every point of industrial life of today.

123. It is common to make idealism antithetical to materialism. There is nevertheless a common movement at the bottom which is deeper than the directions they take. The common movement is the identification of reality with objectivity. Thought must be conceived as objective. But materialism and logical idealism take the standpoint of knowledge as ultimate. The positive organic

view is that things are the mediating reality in activity and that thought is the method of activity. Either abstracted is unreal.

124. It is a common saying that we know only phenomena. But that phrase has two interpretations. A relativity of knowledge is taken to mean that our knowledge is relative to a perfect knowledge, that there is a perfect objective world to which our knowledge is relative. The other means that knowledge as knowledge is phenomenal; it does not define our mode of knowing, but the essential character of knowing itself. The very nature of objectivity is taken to be symbolical. The epistemological idealist analyzing the nature of judgment concludes that judgment as such involves within itself a systematic unity. This is a point of Kant's work. This is where the idealist can always improve the materialist. (See Royce, his Chapters 10 and 11,[12] and Green's *Prolegomena to Ethics*, introductory chapter.)

125. The idealist also sees that this unity is not realized in any particular judgment that we can pass. If "it" is made an object, a contradiction arises. "Of it" says Green, "we can speak only in negatives, can know that it is, but not what it is." The idealist's conclusion leads to the result: an absolute type of thought, of which our knowledge follows after as best it can. The question is whether this conclusion follows from the premises. The conclusion is rather contradictory of the premises. It is not an analysis of our knowledge but of knowledge as knowledge, not in the sense that our knowledge is limited, but in the sense that we know nothing.

126. Then are we to take the opposite solution of agnosticism, and say we are simply limited to appearances and cannot know reality? The difficulty here is the statement of the process of knowledge as ultimate: that experience never gets beyond phenomena. The contradiction is a symbol which does not symbolize, a symbol not one in itself but because it indicates something. If the directive element is taken away they cease to be symbols. The agnostic attempts to have appearances that do not indicate anything but are simply so many facts.

127. From the practical point of view the difficulty is solved by dissolving it. The relativity is in the function, not the content of knowledge. Knowing as knowing is precisely what it pretends to be and is just as good as the absolute knowing. Error does not affect principle. Relativity is fact that is not an end in itself but is fact [in] that it serves purposes. If a spade were criticized not because it was a poor spade but because it is not the process of gardening, the same thing would be done as when knowledge is criticized because it is not an end. The true realization of the relativity of knowledge consists in the use of knowledge as means.

128. What is the unity which the logical idealist finds involved in the judgment as such? Not an absolute object but the act which takes within itself the means as instrument. An object can only indicate a unity; only an act can be a unity. Because our activity is a unity we put unity into everything. An atom is only a working concept. So with a table. The unity is anthropomorphic. When object is set up as a complete unity, the metaphysician can come in and show that it is filled with inconsistencies and contradictions. The real object of science is the use of its phenomena as working. It is as inconsistent to set up a system of a unity as an object. [It is] easier to take an instrument as a complete thing in thought, so that materialism seems more natural. The sense of the abstractness of idealism never leaves one because a method is taken up as a reality.

[Chapter 6. Criticism of the Separation
Between Self and God]

129. Everybody's philosophical thinking is influenced by theological ideas
even if he thinks he has gotten away from the latter. There are images, fundamental schema, still in the mind even of the atheist. In various concepts of God
there are certain views. The difficulties of metaphysical thought are the reflex[13]
of these conflicting views. When we begin to philosophize these contradictions
come. Certain contradictions are involved in ordinary religious training from
which many after problems arise. Even though a man changes the facts as God
and the world, the scheme of connection between God and the world will remain the same. There are historical problems resulting from the method of
treating God as material. The fundamental contradiction is the contradiction
between images impressed on the theoretical side and the motives that are
appealed to in the strictly religious or spiritual consciousness, or contradiction
between methods used and ideals involved.

130. The ideal of Christian consciousness is a life of spiritual unity. It is the
end formulated in the *New Testament*. This is to be [engaged in] some identification, in life, with God. The above is a practical ideal of religious consciousness. The methods used to realize this ideal are largely contradictory to the ideals
themselves. They rest upon a fixed separation between the soul and God. A child
asking where things come from is told "God made them." An image is left on the
child's mind of somebody outside and different who is hard at work.

131. Almost all metaphysical problems on the relation of God to the world
arise out of these early misconceptions. As Kant has pointed out, we cannot
apply cause to the Absolute. The Absolute is contained in all. It is impossible
to apply something to the Absolute outside of time with something inside of
time. The beginning is only relative. It is the beginning of this event; but absolute beginning is without definition. In the Christian concept of Father the
idea of causation is not involved. It is the concept of generation which presupposes the unity, and not of a mechanical maker prior to the mechanical product. In reality children think of one thing from another and not of one thing
made by another. The idea of evolution, as a working method, comes in philosophy before the idea of causation.

132. I have given the religious ideal above. How is that unity of individual will
with [Absolute] will interpreted to the child? Is it interpreted as an end or as
an authority, an authority laying down the end? In psychological analysis of the

will the primary factor in the definition is the end, the ideal, which is to be gained. Force and power come in, but in the means to realize volition. How is it presented in the religious education? Power is not taken as means, but as that which lays down the end. (See *Popular Science Monthly* for the latter half of 1893, [Dewey,] "Present Chaos in Moral Training.")[14]

133. How can we over-bridge this absolute moral break between God as a punisher and the dignified idea of morality? Deism, theism, and pantheism are problems arising from the image of God as an external cause. Theism is simply a vibration between deism and pantheism, taking enough of pantheism to modify the mechanics of deism and enough of deism to keep out of pantheism. Pantheism postulates a unity and, in that, it has done away with dualism, but the dualism is all the time recurring as a semblance at least. But how can the semblance arise in an absolute perfect unified totality? This dualism appears because the unity is objectified and not made a unity of life. The vital, living unity in the world in which all things inhere is far distant from the objective unity. Most philosophical problems arise, then, from an objectified unity or dualism.[15]

The Logic of the Ethical Judgment Proper

[Chapter 7. Interpretation of the Central Moral Categories]

134. [Prior to the occurrence of tension,] every experience begins at a relatively unconscious phase of worth. The next [phase] is where the emphasis is laid upon the process of marking off value; in this the tension occurs and then the unity is rediscovered, but with the tension still conscious.

135. The chief ethical categories ought now to be defined. What do we mean by ethical values? Negative[ly], if this states the logic of judgment, it ought to define the origin of one-sided systems and ought to point out critical places where one is likely to go astray. Again, this logic ought to work both subjectively and objectively so as to apply to individual and social ethics, the presupposition being that the structure and movement are the same in both.

136. Every experience, whether individual or social, develops through these three stages: the logic of the deed, in psychological terms, or of the institutions in social terms.[16] This moral image is typical of the process marking the undifferentiated unity of experience. (·) Certain contradictions arise within the development of experience and the circle becomes an ellipse, one focus standing for subject and the other for predicate. (· ·)The subject, if taken individually, is the habits; socially the institutions and structure already formed. The predicate stands for the future side, the end worked for rather than the acquired law. This tension constitutes for the individual or society its problem. Every moral experience reduces itself ultimately to the problem of unifying ideals with these established habits and life.

137. Psychologically it is a tension between habit, including impulse, and purpose, end, or ideal. The solution will bring the habit and the end into a working unity. The movement from the subject to the predicate sets up the ideal or aim. The predicate moving towards the subject, or the ideal reacting upon the habit, establishes the standard.

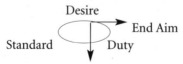

Desire
End Aim
Standard
Duty

Consciousness of duty and of desire are correlative, marking the consciousness of the tension. The habit tries to express itself and sets up an ideal. This reacts upon the habit to reinforce and strengthen it. The former, the duty; the latter, the desire, end. The ideal may stimulate or it may inhibit the habit. The former desire, the latter duty.

138. The thing may be negatively illustrated on the social side by saying that power is conditioned by [an] end. The relative power is determined by conscious or unconscious ideal. The one-sided social theories, Utopias, also illustrate it. Social revolution or anarchism sets up an end which is out of relation to the present power. This is the logic of anarchism. Excessive radicalism negates present power by setting up an end out of relation with it. Ultra conservatism goes to the opposite extreme of holding on to what we have and refusing to use it for any end. The fixed abstraction in these cases is the logic of conservatism and radicalism.

139. An act is gotten which objectively is a solution, the cessation of the tension, and hence a unity; and we get an enlarged circle. Perhaps in the development of this process of moral experience there would be something corresponding to parabola and hyperbola.[17] A congestion of habits is frequently found, as in Egyptian civilization, holding on to all that it had, and continuing empirically without finding laws, as for example, Greece did with Geometry; or in Scholasticism, both in individual and society. It might be objected that these changes are forced from without, not an extending of the circle. A conquest would seem to be external, but that relationship with the conqueror had existed before but had not been realized. A thing cannot get internal adjustments perfected without coming in contact with the external. When the ellipse becomes the enlarged circle we have the realized moral experience. This takes the form of the good; or, negatively, the bad; and also responsibility. These are no longer in antagonism but two phases of the same thing.

140. Before taking up the logic of the [moral] categories there is a question regarding the nature of the whole process. Every stage of it may be interpreted in accordance with empiricist or rationalistic judgment. (Martineau, intuitional; and Mill, empirical side; Dewey, *Syllabus*, p. 88; Mackenzie, [*An Introduction to Social Philosophy*], Chapter IV; Ryland, [*Logic: An Introductory Model for the Use of the University Student*,] Chapter V; Murray, *Introduction to Ethics*, pp. 45–68; Bain, *Emotions and Will*, p. 77; Bain, *Mental and Moral Science*, p. 454.)

[Chapter 8.] The Empirical Theory Concerning Origin and Nature of the Moral Judgment

141. This is but an application of the general logical method. The following implications: (1) observation and collection of special cases, (2) comparison of these cases, (3) induction of a general principle by the calculation of consequences. Certain of our experiences bring pleasure; certain, pain. Empirical logic is always monistic. Having observed a large number of instances, the experiences are collected, compared, as Mill lays down in his *Logic*. We find the common element in experiences leading to pleasure (same for pain) and draw an induction. There is no consciousness of right or wrong in the experiences themselves. Of course, certain things may not be discussed under empirical theory in general, as [the] ideal of [the] hedonists, etc.

142. When it is said that the moral experience is evolved out of the non-moral, it is not meant that the evolution is [in] becoming conscious of moral values in the non-moral experience. They are evolved out of it in the sense that certain external consequences are evolved from the non-moral experience, and by reference to them the experience is moralized.

143. Criticizing the logic [of empiricism] it appears:

(1) The examination of moral experience involves an ideal already implied, to give a basis for observation and classification of experiences. Otherwise the mind would not know which of a multitude of cases to pick out. For example, Darwin must have had some kind of a working hypothesis before he began his work of classification. Otherwise it would simply be found that everything is everything. Thus the empirical logic always begs the question.

(2) The comparison of the cases involves an implicit standard of value; as in observing, there is an ideal. It is the value attached to certain cases, not in the great number of cases collected. On the theoretical side, it is not true that these experiences have the common element. In A, B, C; F, H, C; G, K, C; C is not there obviously. The scientific process consists in discovering the C which is not apparent. If certain qualities had been on the surface, we would not have had to wait for Darwin for the Darwinian hypothesis. The differences left over, A, B; F, H; were explained on the ground of special creation. Evolution does not seek to get other common elements but explains how the differences arose. The identity is defined; the differences are integrated. Thus, empirically, it is most important to know what standard to apply. The unity has to be assumed, but must be allowed to expand to explain differences.

(3) There is always a general relationship between the particular instances and the generality inducted from these instances. It is a common saying that induction can never be certain though a strong presumption may be made. All induction rests on the uniformity of nature. Another supposition, of the uniformity of nature, rests on induction. Thus opposition arises because there is no organic connection between the common element and the divergences. Therefore, it is a matter of chance if the common element is found in the next thousand cases. The fact that we get the practical assurance is because the mind cannot believe but that there is an identity. The scientific man enlarges his universal when he finds an exception. He does not set it aside, but makes it his business to search out the exception. This is unaccountable on the basis of empirical logic.

144. The process in ethics, then, cannot be purely empirical but presupposes a rational factor which directs it. We must know the quality of experience so as to know what kind of knowledge will be derived. This rational factor, the assumption of unity, is itself an assumption. We find by examination that experience is always working toward an end and this is the rational factor. There is an implicit element in experience which, by development, becomes explicit.

145. The moment the non-moral experience becomes conscious itself, it becomes moral. This is the evolution of the moral sense. The biological experience itself is a moral experience; the latter is not simply super-added. Because empiricism is always implying an ideal and a standard, always using a rational element, though denying its existence, the empirical method is always in a state of confusion. The empirical philosophy will always make out a good case but always because a rational element is put in.

146. Ethical empiricism is always alternating between an uncertainty so great as not to be scientific and a fixed rigidity which is unscientific and impracticable. A generalization, such as a command of the decalogue, is supposed to be empirical. Then there is no inherent limitation at all. If murder up to this time has brought more pain than pleasure, how do we know that murder now, in a particular case, will not bring more pleasure than pain? Hence there is a constant temptation to manipulate an uncertainty for justification of things we have already concluded we would like to do. On the other hand, a rigidity results. A crime is simply a violation of a rule, an inherited moral code of race and nation. The sailor uses a nautical almanac simply to help him to realize the particular situation in which he is; he does not seek to bring the particular case under the nautical almanac.[18] It is because of an organic unity that the past cases help in particular cases.

147. Mill defines moral science as an art, not a science. There are certain rules to which present cases must be conformed in order to get rid of uncertainty. The

relationship, being extended, must be subsumed under a given rule. This results [in] a casuistry and we are thrown back on caprice and the tendency to manipulate in our favor. The logic of Jesuitism is in having a lot of rules and in that way comes indecision as to which rule the case will be put under.

148. The practical truth involved in empirical logic is that consciousness of moral truth involves a process of mediation. It is developed and not directly derived. The fact that morality itself demands that moral truth should not be given directly to the mind, appears. Morality would not be morality otherwise. There is no [other?] function of moral experience, no element, in the formation and testing of character than that of working out the moral laws. Without this a person is reduced almost to a machine.[19]

[Chapter 9. Criticism of Intuitionalism]

149. If the intuitional theory were true, all moral experience would reduce itself to applying moral truth to given cases. There would be no responsibility on the individual to discover truth for himself. The intuitional idea is the charitable idea in food and money, also in giving truth—a more important thing. The weakness of intuitionalism is that it does not treat experience as working out the truth.

150. The general contention of intuitionalism is that there must be general and universal truth, not particular or contingent. Experience reveals only the particular. There must then be a power of the mind to realize the universal truths which transcend the particular. It is claimed that you must have a definite starting point, an ultimate truth to which other truths can be carried back. Otherwise there is no certainty anywhere. Of course then, these truths must be immediate, self-evident. Of course, the model of mathematics has been the stronghold of the intuitionalists since Aristotle. There you have axioms.

151. There are three points to be examined: (1) the nature of axioms, (2) deduction of particulars from generals, (3) subsumption.

152. [1] What is meant by self evident truth? If we take the model of mathematics we get a definite question to ask. Does self-evidence consist in the content of the definition as such? Is the straight line between two points gotten from contemplation of content? Or does the self-evidence consist in the fact that we have a process so simplified that the method, and therefore the results, is controlled? Is it opposed to experimental truth or the simplest form of experimental truth? The logic of empiricism is the isolation of a subject, the effort to get a pure case. Does intuitionalism, here, in axioms, do the same? If we take the case of the axiom regarding the straight line, what are we doing? Do we not abstract space from other conditions and then reconstruct space? Is the self-evidence from the simple content of [an] idea as the simplicity of the simple construction we are going through? Is empirical theory regarding geometrical theorems [and] propositions the only alternative to intuitionalism?

153. It is the simplicity of the process of making, constructing, that constitutes the self-evidence of axiomatic truth. There is great difficulty in going from geometrical axioms to ethics. Is the thing that corresponds to this [axiom] certain generalizations[, such] as "murder is wrong"? It is obvious that you are dealing not with simple, but most complex, relations. Instead of enabling you to reconstruct that complete society, it gives you simply truisms that are not fertile, and do not go on as axiomatic truths.

154. [2] The question here is, "Is it not possible to reduce moral experience to its simplest elements and conditions and then get a starting point which will not be truistic, but a purification as we have in time and space relations?" There is no necessary impossibility here, and it must be done if we are to get a science of ethics, by deduction as consisting in derivation of particular from general truths. No one ever did this. A general truth simply remains general. If we attempt to image any state of things corresponding to the statement it will be found impossible. We have particular mathematical truths demonstrated with reference to axioms, but they are not derived from any general truths. There is no absolute, essential, difference between a definition and a demonstration. Some geometries take as axioms what others take as demonstrations.

155. There is no process of drawing a particular from a general truth. The important point is always the auxiliary construction from the primary construction. The former is not drawn from the latter; the latter is simply another demonstration under simpler conditions. If this holds in geometry it will hold anywhere else. The real process, then, is not a deduction, but such a use of the general with regard to the particular as to organize the latter into a comprehensive whole.

156. The correlative of this, the assumption, according to intuitionalism, is always given. This process always means loss. We are always losing something from the reality of the case. The old classifications were subsumptions. The interest was simply in putting a particular case in a given pigeon-hole. The differences of a particular are then lost, disregarded. There is loss on both sides. The universal does not grow. The particular is not taken in the concrete wealth which it has.

157. The difficulty in intuitionalism is how to subsume the particular under the general. The intuitionalists have been forced to make their intuitions more and more general. Not this particular case of killing is wrong, but simply that murder is wrong. And some, like Kant, go further back and say the only intuition is that of obligation in general. When you get to this point, of what use is your intuition, for every case of conduct is a particular case.

158. The whole essence, then, lies in the ability to relate the general principles to the particular case, but it does not show the way they are to be related. Therefore the method lends itself, at least as fully as empiricism, to casuistry. The universal has no differentiating power because it is this immediate thing.

159. Practically speaking, empiricism has been an ethics of progress, intuitionalism of conservatism. The intuitionalist will pick out the moral standards of his own time. This has its good side in lending a stable element, and its bad side in becoming rigid and withdrawing itself from criticism and setting a fixed

barrier to progress. Empiricism has always lent itself to progress. It has been an ethics of political reform, for example, Locke, Bentham. On the one hand empiricism cannot generalize its own method, and since it cannot set up an end it cannot define the means. The inability to formulate a working universal causes fluctuations and uncertainty. The truth of intuitionalism is that moral truth is intrinsic and objective, but it perverts this by claiming that the mind can immediately grasp it. Its fault is the strength of empiricism. The two schools are correlative to each other.

160. The logic, as against the one-sidedness of empiricism, is an experimental idealism. The experimental process should not be confounded with the empirical process; for the former sets up a unity and by it controls the empirical process. On the other hand this unity which the experimental process asserts is not a fixed thing. It is not asserted for itself but as a working hypothesis for the organization of the empirical process. This method is beyond and below both systems. The true logic is the logic of an experimental idealism.

161. There can be no opposition between the categories of objective experience and the categories of moral experience. On the one side is the contention that Ethics is a deductive *a priori* science, essentially at least a psychological science. On the other, that it is an historical inductive science, or at least it is a purely sociological science. One or the other of these presumptions underlies almost every treatise on the science of ethics.

162. The defect in the latter is that it leaves us at the mercy of opinion regarding the organizing principles. Every science is not a mere collection of facts. This method gives us no clue [about how] to pick out and classify particular facts. The result is that the individual is at the mercy of his own hobby, [his] conscious or unconscious prejudices, and becomes utilitarian. There is also something implied but not made explicit in the subject-matter itself, but there is no way to examine the implied ideals and find out how they are generated. The material itself is psychological; and unless we have worked out the psychology of experience when it took place, there is no way to use it historically. The valuable results of this method have come because some men who used historical material have had sound psychological principles.

163. Then to have the psychology in and of itself is to have the method of interpretation without the facts. The intuitionalist sets up the method as intuitional and defeats its own end. There is no psychological process which does not express itself historically, just as much today as two thousand years ago. The psychological process is not complete until an act takes place in space and time. The false separation of the inner and the outer, the subjective and objective, underlies the confusion.

164. Then the need of ethical science is, first, an adequate psychology which shall point out the outline, [which will] give us the skeleton of any particular experience [as] ethical. The adequate detailed historical knowledge [is] interpreted, then, in the light of the working hypothesis which the psychological analysis supplies. The need of Ethics is precisely what the need of Zoology was when the first generalizations of comparative anatomy were made. Comparative anatomy was not simply an examination of a lot of animals, but an idea of animal life manifesting itself in various special forms which was used in the examination of animal life. The separation in Ethics is what we have in Biology if we separate the facts from the theory of evolution. We must know the facts but we get the science by interpreting the facts in reference to our theory of evolution.

165. The so-called deductive principle is the interpreting and organizing, while the inductive or historical furnishes the material which has to be interpreted and valued. This distinction is simply a division of labor in the development of science itself. In the subject-matter there is but one living process. There is no separation in the reality. What we call the universal is the aspect of the reality which is fruitful in revealing to us as yet unknown phases of the reality. It is *a priori* in function and not in principle.

166. The other element, induction *a posteriori*, is that aspect of reality which serves to concrete, to objectify our working hypothesis. The two are correlative because they are but phases of one process. The law of gravitation is *a priori* when used to interpret facts, *a posteriori* if studied in historical development and worked out in special detail. So [it is] with the hypothesis of evolution.

167. Spencer, in his induction of ethics, fails to give a psychological interpretation of historical data. He gives valuable facts, but fails in scientific treatment. They are put under various heads as though that constituted a scientific classification.

168. The facts as given are not real facts, but indications of facts. The particular fact has to be placed in the whole social landscape. It is a function of the social life. We have to know the whole social organization of the people from whom the illustrations are taken. When the fact is placed in its social bearings we will necessarily get the psychology of it if we have a fair psychological hypothesis to begin with. When we feel the need of explaining and understanding a fact, we have not got the fact itself in its entirety. It may be good so far as it goes but not able to stand alone. It may be called *a* fact but not *the* fact.

169. The real scientific process is the building up of the fact itself. It does not lie outside the fact. The recalled facts or data of science are really the problem of science. The scientific process is not explaining facts, but substituting recon-

structed facts for incomplete facts. This result always reacts and transforms the premises. If the hypothesis is changed, the facts are changed. The theory in physics is so well defined that the facts can be taken as established when they are collected. In some other sciences it cannot be known that facts will be of any value when they are gotten, because the theories are not so well defined. The fluid facts and the hypothesis are correlates.

170. Spencer does not use his own psychology or even his biology in relation to the particular facts which he advances. This indicates the necessity of some further advance in ethical science. In his sociology he indicates all primitive peoples are very callous. In his ethics he is an hedonist. Yet he never sees the inconsistency in his system when he claims that his system points to optimism.

[Chapter 10. The Logic of the Formation of Ideals]

171. One of the most obvious phenomena of life is the apparent disjunction of the actual and the ideal. And the testing point of every ethical system is how it accounts for the splitting up of the ethical experience into the "is" and the "might be." In Psychology, the logic of actual and ideal would be applied to impulse and progress; in Politics, the positive laws and natural laws; [while] in Political Economy, supply and demand.

172. The origin of this distinction [is that] a given cycle of experience gets overloaded or congested. The principle or method on which that activity is being conducted is reflected in results, and these results are continually increasing in number. A given civilization works it out into the details of actual life. These results harmonize for a time (as the classical period of Greek life) and there is no consciousness of any break. The results accumulated to the extent that they overload the principle, and distinctions arise in the activity itself.

173. The Ptolemaic theory worked out its own destruction. Newly observed facts were brought into the theory and it broke down. The picture of the universe became so complex that it could not be carried. The implicit method of Greek life worked itself out in results that were too much for it. Socrates was the best product of the Greek life. In him the results worked out were too much for it and the result was his death. The continual research and discussion were essential elements of Greek life. Every proposal was brought before the assembly before it was made law. But the Greek social life could not stand becoming conscious of itself.

174. So in Plato and Aristotle the theory and the life are set over against each other. Plato tries to harmonize [them], while Aristotle virtually states there is a dualism in the distinction between the universal and the particular (which marked the whole scholastic philosophy). A working reconstruction for the whole system resulted. Socrates took it for granted that the universal was in life and attempted to show it. Later theory got the right to theorize by saying it would not attempt to apply itself to life.[20]

175. It is the very nature of experience to have these critical points where the working of it out becomes so elaborate that it must be reconstructed.[21] These critical points of reconstruction are essential and intrinsic in all experience. The getting of the new power cannot be simply cumulative and quantitative, e.g., the appearance of the eye so enlarges the world of the animal that it has to readjust all other organs. The possession of the eye is not simply a privilege. The art of photography grew out of old arts, but has required a readjustment of old arts.

176. The distinction between the actual and ideal arises out of and because of this necessity of reconstruction. Something now has to be done because of the accumulated details. Except at these times the ideal is actualized and there can be no split. The split arises because, when these accumulations become so numerous, it is necessary to reflect (a complication of the activity compels it) and this reflection polarizes or dualizes experience. The "stopping to think" is the actual thinking. When friction arises, it is a sign that you should stop and reflect.

177. How does the distinction arise through reflection? The reflection is an inventory. Its first question is, "What are the actual conditions?" There is set up on one side the status, the state of things, which is obviously equivalent to acquisitions, which are our resources in this particular case. It represents past accomplishment, what has been done. It is not present therefore, not the ultimate reality. What we term the actual, as distinguished from the ideal, consists of the resources at [our] command, of the realized accomplished state of things: that arising through reflection, which arises through conflict or friction.[22]

178. What is the ideal? When we reflect upon experience as a whole and set before us objectively a certain state of things, the subject drops out. There is projection on one side and withdrawal on the other. The very fact that we reflect on experience means that we make an abstraction. Now that which is left out is not destroyed, but reappears in another form as the subject. To define the stream you must stop it, and take a cross-section. The movement does not usually stop. This is a device for defining the activity. The feeling of that formal movement as distinct from the movement up to date constitutes the ideal.

179. The student graduating stops and reflects upon his acquirements. Because he is doing that, there is a consciousness of something ahead with reference to which he must use his resources. Here is the self as it has accomplished [something], brought up just short of the date. And therefore there is a tension, a sense of work yet to be done, a consciousness that this self is not the whole self. Or, if he is not able to define the end which will utilize his resources, the more dissatisfied he feels with his resources, the more he feels that he has been cheated in his experience up to date. Thus the tension is brought out in a pathological form.

180. The life impulse never stops. So long as there is no friction there is no sense of break; but if the friction comes in it feels that what it has accomplished is an obstacle to what it should accomplish. The life process is the permanent thing. As the actual side becomes defined as an object, the impulse side becomes defined as an ideal.

181. Wherever there is a movement of projection which results in the object, there is a movement of introjection which results in the subject. The action and reaction are equal because they are two sides of the same process. The act of exchange sets up a buyer and a seller. There is one process which you look at from

one or the other side, supply and demand. The act of reflection is not to be conceived of as if there were a subject and an object there. A movement is set up which is on the one side a movement of withdrawal and on the other of projection. It is the same self.

182. In regard to temperance reform, here is a certain waste of social powers, resulting in crime and poverty. This constitutes a reflection on the friction. The definiteness with which the ideal is conceived will be exactly correlative with the definiteness with which the facts are perceived. Friction itself sets up this polarity of movement. If you abstract a phase of the facts, the ideal becomes equally partial. If you abstract simply [the] act of alcohol or poison, your ideal is to do away with it. If the perception of facts is extended to poorly housed, overworked people, the ideal will be extended to amelioration of their condition. The conception will become a working hypothesis with reference to which facts are gathered thereafter, either of crime, etc., for the prohibitionist or of industrial conditions for the person interested in social and industrial reform.

183. Nothing but a recognition of the movement of society will overthrow those evils. The movement that has produced them will be the power which can be utilized to reconstruct them. The movement of the state of things, and the state of things [themselves], are set up against each other in reflection. This would be a harmful thing if it were not a normal phase in the evolution of experience.

184. What happens when an ideal is set up which is not the movement of the facts themselves? Taken out of the facts, it has no leverage in the facts and is helpless. If the movement is radically wrong it is impossible to get any leverage on it to make it revolve. Nothing but a supernatural miracle would effect any change.

185. When the idea is isolated and abstracted there is this impotency, the self-contradiction of abrupt revolution. There construction of the past is in some sense a revolution. Every reform, social or industrial, involves such a revolution. But the catastrophic revolution, e.g., the French, is an oscillation and not a revolution. The parts of the revolution which succeeded were those in the direction of which society was already moving. The others failed.

186. The concept is simply a method of reconstruction. It is not an object to be realized. It is a method of activity and not a thing. The image of the ideal as something to be realized has a strong hold on the human mind, because Ethics is now in the condition which science was in medieval times.

187. Reality is always a moving state of things. The ideal is of no more value than the actual. When the ideal is isolated, it is not only impotent, but harmful; it leads to the attempt of impossible things and brings evil, as in the French

revolution. The moral fruit of this is a sort of Pharisaism. It is regarded as a sort of possession to be enjoyed. It does not refer itself to concrete work and injures the moral motive.[23]

188. False conservatism is no worse than a false idealism. The tendency to set up these vast schemes leads to a withdrawal. "I," as having this ideal, "am good, the rest are bad." The ideal is just as bad as the state of things if it is abstract in character. Such persons take the test of the ideal to be the extent to which it will stir their emotions, not because of what they will accomplish. It is not because the idea is general that it fails, but because it has been arrived at by a reaction from existing conditions.

189. Ethical theory is an abstraction from ethical experience as such, and in getting that general movement it gives a standard for criticism and [for] reconstruction of the existing movement. (See [Dewey], *International Journal of Ethics*, Vol. I.)[24] Between this and the special ideals there are obviously a number of intermediate ideals such as justice, chastity, etc. The ideal, for example, of justice, is not a useless ideal. Most people will assume that they know what justice is. That vague concept of justice is worse than useless, because it is acted upon. A person holding it is at the mercy of his own feelings or the traditions received from his teachers. There should be first a mastery of the actual facts to discuss what the actual movement of these facts is.

190. How can the ordinary ideal of justice help in the application of justice to industrial trusts? One must first find the trend of industrial forces. There must be some theory of interpretation, a theory of ethical movement of society as a whole as an ethical organization. And we must see what the relation of this movement is to the whole organism. This requires patience, so it seems easier to do something at once.

191. The value of general ideals is then to be simply the theory. (See Spencer on Absolute and Relative Ethics.)[25] The absolute right would be the action that brought pleasure, and pleasure only, to all concerned. He takes an example from the progress of a mechanism or formula regarding the lever, and shows how this is worked out by empirical facts. The theory of mechanics presupposes conditions in which there is no friction. Just as actual mechanics start from ideal theories and make allowances for friction, so in ethical life the ideal may be formed. Then, the allowances can be made and the relatively right determined.

192. The philosophical moralists treat of the absolutely straight man. The actual experience marks a deviation from the absolute ideal. Is this interpretation required by an analogy from mechanics? Does the theory of mechanics represent the absolute goal in comparison with a defective state of things? Could the mechanic get a mechanics that would work if he got these ideal conditions? No

machine could ever work that conformed to these conditions. No energy could be transmitted. There is a moral ideal like a point of view, like a machine has, or a goal to be reached. An ideal is an intellectual point of view from which to reflect upon the state of things, not a goal to be reached. The ideal becomes at once a motive. It is intellectual simply while you are defining your hypothesis. But when the latter is formed it becomes a motive or basis for experimentation.

193. We have two ways in which the ideal may be objectified, from the standpoint of subject or predicate. The ideal as a goal to be reached may be regarded as pleasure or perfection, as one or the other is taken. Moral life is held to be tending toward pleasure or perfection. The logic of hedonism and of perfection have a common basis, the ideal is something to be reached. Neither holds that the ideal is a theory for ordering present conditions. Both think that the goal can never be reached or at least involves more change in existing conditions than we can conceive of before it can be reached. Yet most hedonists think that a surplus [of pleasure] over pain is the realization of the ideal.

194. The ideal [is] involved in the idea of limit which is a true conception, but is here in Spencer and others misinterpreted. Both hedonism and perfection conceive of the goal as something to be attained and both require conditions which can never be expected in this world. It is the function of an ideal to serve as a limit for action. But is it an objective thing? According to our use it has to be conceived as having a function. The ethical ideal outlines the scope within which the action falls.

195. How far shall an impulse to relieve suffering be followed? On reflection, intellectual limits are set up for activity within which this one falls. The scope is defined before we let the impulse pass over into overt action. Often having started out [with] a certain plan, and obstacles arise, [yet] we go on doing it in spite of the obstacles. When we follow an impulse another activity tends to carry us into other fields, the ideal has the function of warning us.

196. The term 'ideal' may be changed to 'plan,' and this appears clearer. When we have a plan it seems to mark the outline of our activity; it indicates that certain things are to be left out. The ideal sets certain channels, preferred to others, along which the activity is to flow, and allows one to economize his effort. Unless definition is a physical thing it must mean selecting activity, an emphasis for which certain points are selected. So the ideal reduces itself to consciousness of one line of action as performed. Its function is to let us know what we are about by holding our activity in coherency.

197. The logic of criticisms of hedonism rests on the perception that pleasure as realized is never the ideal. If the ideal is actual pleasure it is not an ideal.

Hedonism has to set up a thought of pleasure. The concept of pleasure has to be developed until you get the greatest sum of pleasures. There is no such thing. It is an absolute abstraction. It is taken as a point of view from which we interpret the activity. Taken as a guide it has a sense, but has no sense taken in any other way. (Cf. Dewey, *Outlines of Ethics*.)[26] Theoretically, pleasure is set up as feeling, as an ideal; but the very fact that it is an ideal makes it the thought of pleasure. Pleasure is often set up as the only alternative to hedonism.[27]

198. Kant and Green best state the theory of perfection as the moral ideal. Protestant perfectionism defines the ideal as something outside the self. Kant makes the perfected will take the place of an objective ideal. (Dewey, *Philosophical Review*, I and II for criticism on Green.)[28] On one side the concept of the completed self and on the other of capacity as something to be realized. The self according to Green is the comprehensive unity. This self makes use of [the] organism in space and time as a vehicle through which to manifest and realize itself. The self has wants and has objective consciousness of wants, the consciousness of an ideal. Not only are we moved on by the impulse of hunger to food, but we know we are hungry.

199. But does the reaching of that end realize the unity of the self? No, for the satisfaction of no particular want would be adequate to complete self-realization. The whole self is not particular. We become conscious of the need of satisfying the want of the whole self as distinguished from the satisfaction of particular wants, and this becomes the ideal. It cannot be realized in any state of life of which we have had experience.

200. The nerve of this argument is in the assumption of the unity of the self. Thus we are worse off than animals, because not having consciousness of their self as a whole, they set up no ideal over against the particular satisfactions, and they are thus conscious of no break. We are sufficiently conscious of the unity of the self to condemn every particular satisfaction, but we can never attain the completed self which is the ideal. Given an all-comprehensive self, why should it set up a vehicle of realization which does not carry it anywhere? Either the self is limited by conditions under which it must realize itself, or for some inexplicable reason, this self chooses to work with space and time conditions.

201. What is the relation of identity to difference? Here we have the setting up of unity against the manifold. The unity of the self is set up as a unified self. Any real unity, in logic, is a present working, functional unity. Green has abstracted this unity and made it the objectified, unified self. This unity of the self is an ideal in the sense that it is a standpoint from which to organize the present activity. However we act, we must so act as to realize the unity of the self.

The limits are thus set up. Therefore, whatever conditions are involved in this unity must be involved in particular actions. The abstraction arises in setting up the unity of the self as an object, as a goal.

202. The unity is never a far away thing to be realized, but [it is] to be realized in this particular act. No act is moral unless it has a definite end, but this definite end must express the unity. The definite end is the special functioning in this special direction. The significance of a moral act is that we realize the whole in this special act.

203. The side of definiteness and the side of unity are related as follows: The specific or definite is an expressing of the fact that the unity is not aimless but always has a focus, an outcome; while unity expresses the fact that this specific outcome always has an organizing principle, is not chaotic. In the process, the difference and the unity fall apart. Each of these is then an abstraction. One is the percept of difference; the other is the concept of unity. When the activity actually occurs, the difference amounts simply to the fact that the unity has a definite focus.

204. The ultimate generalization of the ideal as movement is the unity of the self. Then the function of the abstraction of the movement is to enable us to put value in the analysis of the act. When the ideal is regarded not as the abstraction of the movement of the whole but as an objective something to be realized, the logical abstraction results.

205. When the ideal is set up on the one side, what is its opposite? The movement falls into conditions on the one side and the method or ideal on the other. What has been taking place is consciousness of conditions as the consciousness of ideal is growing.

206. As the conditions are interpreted in terms of the ideal, what evolution do they go through? They become less and less the more static "conditions as attained facts," and become thought of as capacities or possibilities. (An impossibility is an attained fact interpreted in the light of the ideal.) Correlative with the growth of the ideal in consciousness, the conditions are thought of as potentialities in connection with the future instead of the past activities. The more we measure accomplishments in the light of the ideal, the more they appear in consciousness as urging on, as impelling to future activity.

207. With Kant and Green, if this ideal is regarded as [an] objective goal, that conception reflects itself back into the conditions. The present self must be conceived in some way as affording the capacities for realizing the idea. In the other case, capacity is dynamic, power-capacity. In this [case,] capacity, possibility, is static. Here we think of capacity as a lack. [There is] nothing in the measure itself by which it gets filled. Here a possibility means simply that it is not real.

The capacities have to be interpreted as the possible filling of the objective goal. Yet the "more"[29] measure holds so much that it can never be filled. The separate capacities are unrealized, an empty possibility for us, though realized in God.

208. On Green's theory the individuals could realize the ideal only as they lost their differences, and became all like each other because they were all like the infinite self. This leaves no place for the social element. There would be no individuality but millions of duplicates.

209. When you say a person has certain capacities, you mean that the activities are there, urgent for expression. The process of interpreting the activity sets up the capacity on the one side and the ideal on the other. On the theory of the objective ideal the statement that a child has an engineering capacity which ought to be developed is meaningless. The capacity must be absolutely the present power. The value of the ideal is to point out a wider reality than was present before.

210. The logical fallacy comes in when this distinction of value is made into separate existences. There is only one reality, one existence, and the differentiations are only in valuations. If we break the latter, the two set-over things appear, which can never be brought together.

211. The formation of the ideal involves a reflective process, though the ideal presents itself as an active dynamic thing. When we discuss moral standards there is obviously a process of reflection. The standard is the ideal taken in its reflective or mediative aspect. We take the ideal to determine the values of actions, and it becomes a standard. Thus there is an organic unity of the standard and the ideal.

212. Both hedonists and perfectionists make a break between them. Pleasure is the ideal but not the standard. The attainment of the pleasure does not measure the moral value of the act. The act as contributing to the happiness of all mankind or all sentient creatures is judged the right one. Høffding realizes better than any other hedonist the break.[30]

[Chapter 11. Standards as Perfection in the Practical Sense]

213. Can perfection be taken as a standard for measuring a particular act? We cannot measure the length of finite space by infinite space. Neither [can we measure] a particular act by perfection. Green recognized the break. He said we should ask if this particular act were [to be] measured by the objectification of the infinite ideal, which is brought up to date. But can this objectification be a reliable measure? Is not the relation rather a negative one? It appears that the present institution must be done away with because it is not in harmony with the ideal. If we can trust to the objectification of the infinite in existing social institutions, why not also its objectification in our instincts?

214. According to Green the infinite self cannot be conceived of in terms of our own consciousness. It is only an infinite goal. So far the social objectification has come only to a certain point. (See Green's analysis of the comparative values of Christian and Greek standards.)[31] As the area extends its virtue, it extends qualitatively, as from the physical temperance of the Greek to the self-sacrifice of the Christian. Green then simply analyzes the actual movement and defines the ideal in relation to the actual movement. He does not show how the infinite goal shall be applied to a particular case.

215. Because the infinite goal is everything, it is not a workable standard. The goal is infinitely remote. You cannot measure the finite by it. When you have attained to a given point, because the goal is infinitely remote, you cannot tell whether you have gone forward or backward. According to the other theory, when you have attained to a given point, you must follow a new ideal because you have gotten more material, [more] capacity, and the movement tends to go on and realize the new ideal.

216. The ideal never presents itself as a standard. Where there is simply one ideal, that ideal would be the objective standard. But there can never be one ideal. Because the ideal rises from tension there will be two suggestions, though one ideal would be so slight as to be almost overlooked. Having two ideals you must get a standard to find out which of the two suggested ideals is the real ideal. That ideal which is selected as *the* ideal is the standard. That standard is perfection. That ideal which will resolve this conflict of ideals is perfection in the practical sense of the term, as distinguished from the metaphysical sense.

217. The final ideal which becomes the standard grows from the ideals stimulated by the organic tension. There is no consciousness of value except through the tension of suggested ideals. Psychologically the activity includes the other

ideals as well as the actual ideal. The value of the latter is constituted from the other ideals out of which it rises. The man who has not stolen after being tempted, acts upon a standard which includes the stealing. The man who has not stolen because he has never been tempted, has not selected an ideal.

218. This tension between the ideals constitutes the scale of value. The standard is the good. The standard applied constitutes the right. The ideal developed is no longer merely an end but is the good. This, applied, is the right.

219. The ambiguity about perfection comes from identifying perfection with the top of the scale of values instead of resolving the tension. The capacities consolidated are the agent. The ends consolidated are the ideal, or object, for the agent.

220. Things as known are outside of the subject as knower. In this sense ideals are objective. The ideal is just as real as the agent. The formation of the ideal in general is from these partial ideals. These particular ideals are related to the ideal as parts to a whole. Perhaps it would be better to say the former are suggestions of ideals, while the ideal is in process of formation. Each of these suggested ideals is an ideal so far as it goes, but cannot become the ideal until it controls action.

221. The idea of a scale or hierarchy of values necessarily goes along with the idea of standard. The final object of a standard is to compare various acts as suggested ideals with each other. A common denominator of value is not to be used to measure a given act absolutely. The first object of a standard is to give a basis for determining the values of the different suggested courses of action. We cannot compare one suggested ideal with another in terms of these suggested ideals themselves. You compare one line with another by dividing both into given units, [such as] inches.

222. It is as if an umpire were appointed to decide between the suggested ideals. But the umpire or standard is not a third thing which is brought in, but is the mediation of the conflicting ideals themselves. It comprehends in its organic value the special values of the various suggested lines of action, just as an arbitrator is supposed to take into consideration both sides and not to arbitrarily take one side. A partial idea would function the self, but in such a way as to result in friction. A complete ideal functions the self within itself.

223. Right and wrong have so long been presented to us in objective ways that they have become materialized. One must be chosen, the other rejected. This idea of the standard does not involve the rejection of either.

224. A child at the beginning is either originally depraved or its first impulses are without moral value. Where then can the line be drawn where the child's impulses have moral value? We must either say the final standard comprehends all

the ideals without a psychological exclusion or else the impulses have no psychological value. Is the impulse of anger to be suppressed or utilized and functioned by having some other end set up before it? Anger indicated some kind of force. If suppressed you may break down the strongest element in the child's character. The functioning of the impulse would mean the mediation of it so that the impulse would be so widened that the obstacles which seem to present themselves at the outset should be used as stimuli.

225. I meet [up with an] impulse to steal. The distinction of *meum* and *tuum*[32] should not be [seen as] an arbitrary device of society, but as a means of functioning the impulse. If private property is set up as a means of evolving this instinct, the child should be shown that distribution is necessary. The realization of freedom requires the institution of private property. If the institution is only arbitrary the child should grow up to be a communist. Physically, the resulting action may agree with one of the impulses, but psychologically it comprehends all the impulses and results from reflection. Psychologically, the tension gives the key to the whole thing. This is usually expressed by saying it is the spirit in which a thing is done. What we want to do is to think of acts as the direction of attention, instead of thinking of them on the external side.

226. The most radical defect in the training of children is that the act is materialized. Only the certain physical means of suppression of excitation are gotten, instead of finding ways of directing attention. The standard has to give the sphere of action in which the special ideals operate. The scale of value will not be in consciousness until a certain maturity has been reached.

227. In the race as we find it there always have been generalizations and habits. If the habit is brought to consciousness we have the standard. The most fundamental and comprehensive habit brought to consciousness is the standard. At any moderate degree of progress these habits have come to consciousness. In such a case the standard is not worked out with reference to the results of previous experience.

228. We use these standards of reference to compare the various suggested lines of action in a particular case. When we do so we say they are good, better, best. This standard derived from past experience is the general movement of the self. In this scale one is labeled best. Then it is not what it was before, not an impulse. The other impulses have come in as mediating background, as contributing to the best. A cross-section of the various elements of the scale of values is the old; the movement is the new. The standard is not derived *from* past experience but is formulated *on* past experience.

229. The application of the standard to particular cases develops the standard itself. The very application of the standard or habit changes or develops it. A

child does not know what a foot rule is until he measures certain objects with it. So also in learning the value of a dollar. The standard is always in-process-of-development-through-its-application. Thus there is never a fixed standard of money. The standard is always reformulated on the basis of present experience, though formulated on the basis of past experience. Thus morality is the realization of self.

230. The fact that a standard is recognized by morally advanced people does not justify the presentation of it in an abstract way to another, less advanced people. To assert the standard in general without attempting to interpret it through the experience of the lower class is Pharisaism.

231. On the other hand, there should be an ethical division of labor. There is no reason why those who come at the eleventh hour should not get the benefits of the moral labors of those who have preceded them. They should be brought to the realization of the ideal without being compelled to go through the painful and long process by which the more advanced have gotten their standard. No one exactly parallels the experience of another. But if there is a common nature, the experience of the more advanced may be used to interpret the experience of the less advanced. Unless the higher standard is interpreted, it is but Pharisaism to present moral maxims and standards to others.

232. The applicability of a standard under different circumstances is a test of the standard. If there is a common humanity and the standard cannot be applied among all peoples, there is something wrong with the standard.

233. It is impossible to ignore the influence upon the standard itself of the historical development [of the standard]. It is impossible, for example, to return to the Christian standard of the first century because the standard has been growing all the time. The real conception of perfectionism is a stage in determining the good. Morally, the good is better than the best. The recognition of the suggested ideal which becomes the true good in the scale [of goods] is an aesthetic conception. The best, or perfection, is always a concrete thing and not an abstraction. It is the organization of the given self and not of the remote self.

234. Practically, the determination of the best in the concrete calls forth the greatest moral energy, while the attempt to attain to the abstract perfection is vague and unsatisfactory. "Be perfect as your Father in heaven is perfect." This is not a call to abstract perfection, but the first clause is interpreted by the second. The fatherhood of God means an organic spiritual relationship. The command must then be interpreted through this organic spiritual relationship. This term is the best that could be chosen for the purposes.

235. It is mere truism to say that "unless a person does the best under the circumstances he can never realize the abstract perfection." The objection to the

phrase is that it does not express the organic relationship to the best [extent]. The end which is followed comprehends the others; hence it is not a compromise, but a resolution of the forces which are acting.

236. Perfection comes in as an hypothesis. It has the value which any general abstraction has, to negate the immediacy of the situation and to enable one intellectually (not practically) to get off and get a viewpoint for reflection. It is like climbing a mountain to see what is all around you. It is not like a goal to be attained, but enables you to come down and act according to the concrete circumstances.

237. The concept of perfection means simply how deep down a person goes in interpreting his experience. The scale is determined through tension. (For opposite view see Martineau's hierarchy of springs to action.)[33] Any formulated scale of values represents a scale of ends rather than of the impulses themselves. Again, the respective values of these ends never have an absolute fixity, though relatively at a certain time there may be. Relative fixity means that our past experience has given us tools ready to use, but the order [of the ends] is constantly subject to revision. Indeed, there is a moral responsibility to subject them [the ends] to revision.

238. The part played by tension in evolving the consciousness of standards of measurements and scales of measures needs more attention than has been given it. "There is no progress except the consciousness of progress." If this is true you must pay the cost of the tension or conflict in order to get the consciousness. If appreciation is psychologically conditioned on tension, you must have the tension. If there is no tension between suggested impulses, [so] that we could get everything we want at once, would there be any basis for determining the respective values of these impulses? Could you consciously say that any one of them was good at all? Unless you have some conflict between respective impulses, you cannot compare them at all. If each is an end, it is neither better nor worse. If they are means to an end they may be measured. If persons could ever have had all the land they wanted, no one would ever have measured land. So [it is] with weighing of food and measuring time. It is because, first, immediate conflict and, second, the necessity of adjusting the impulses, that we measure and get any consciousness of a scale of worths.

239. The conflict is in thought and not in action. Conflict in action leads to friction and waste. The transfer of the conflict to thought constitutes the consciousness of good. Whatever good has come from war has been found in the transfer of the conflict to consciousness. The work done by war always has to be

done over again in consciousness, and is harder to do then because of the waste from our physical conflict, e.g., the moral problem of freeing the slaves has to be solved after the war is over. The defeated side usually gets the greater benefit because the transfer then takes place into the region of thought. When a conflict has become physical it shows that the intellectual conflict has not been completed. War takes place because of impatience, and the short cut has to be paid for in the end.

240. All arguments for pessimism which rest on the disunity between thought and will have no force unless it can be shown that these conflicts do not function in any way to bring about deeper good. If the conflicts lead to sheer waste, pessimism holds. The nerve of the pessimistic argument rests on an objective good that has been set up. The opposition is a necessary element in the recognition of value. It also modifies the conception of optimism. It regards the best as the superlative degree of the good, instead of regarding the good as the positive degree of the best. If it is shown (as in Leibniz) that this is the best possible world, it is the only possible world. The good is here purely objective. If meliorism is taken, the same question arises. Is the comparative degree any more satisfying than optimism? Bonism seems to be the right term. The movement of life is good. Better comes in, not in getting something absolutely better, but in freeing the tendency of the movement. If the movement is good that has to be realized. It is not a question of substituting something for the present but in freeing the present.

241. What is the relationship of the concept of good and bad to the concept of right and wrong? The former have been used in determining values of the various ideals. The end becomes the ideal which differentiates itself into best, better, worse, etc., which gives rise to the good, the standard. In addition to the end we have the present impulse or habit. The question is to adjust an impulse and habit to each other. It is to value the conflict of the impulse that we formulate the ideal. Having found what the good is, we come back to our impulses and determine their values. To satisfy this impulse would be wrong, to satisfy that [one] would be right. The concepts are one and the same category applied to the general as good and bad, and then to the particular as right and wrong. This is the reason why all terms for right and wrong have the etymological meaning of conformity to law. The categories of the standard and [of the] law are the same.

242. The fallacies about law arise in the same way as the fallacies about the standard, by considering law as something objective to be conformed to. The law is simply the standard in operation.

243. To say that a thing conforms to the law means it will stand the test of the application of the standard. The law is not a fixed thing outside of the self nor an unchanging thing within the self. Does the particular act fall into the movement of the self and further that movement, or hinder it and cause conflict? The true universal in science is neither a fixed fact nor a fixed law, but the true application of the particular.

[Chapter 12. Badness and Negative Judgment]

244. What is the nature of the negative judgment? On the theory above developed we cannot work from the ideal bad back to the act [as] wrong. No person ever followed any end as evil. The process of finding out the end is the process of finding the good. Nobody ever chooses an end as bad. What a man does is what his real judgment of the good is.

245. The real difficulty is said to be to get the will to accept what is intellectually perceived as good. But this conventional, second-hand recognition of good (moral recognition of good) has to pass over into action. The end and the good are always synonymous terms. The act has to work back from the ideal good.

246. The Socratic theory was easily recognized by the Greeks because they did not have the mass of material, books, etc., that we have. Then, the conception of knowledge was different. Knowledge, then, meant not information but the getting hold of things. Juvenal and later moralists had an accumulated store of knowledge to fall on. The Greek had only his life to fall back on. The act of realizing the supreme value and the act of choice are the same things. Socrates's interest was in showing that impulse-action was non-moral. We must say, with this theory, that a man had a good end and his act was evil.

247. In science how do we determine that a certain proposition is false? Is it because of falsity or truth that we determine the falsity of a particular statement? The discovery of falsity is not the discovery of inherent falsity but the application of the truth. Then the really good man is most conscious of badness. The badness of the bad man ultimately consists in the fact that he is not conscious of it. The test of goodness is the ability to detect badness. The end, when acted on, reveals the goodness or badness of the act. The end sought as end is always the good. Therefore we cannot determine the wrong by subsuming it under the end.

248. The act is the complete concrete approbation, the completed judgment. The act both tests and determines the value. Because the act is the completed judgment it always transcends both subject and predicate. It is a new organization of experience in which the ideal is verified through new material and has therefore grown. Every act therefore, in setting up a new situation or organizing a new self, gives a basis for judging the previous subject and predicate. The good as acted upon throws light upon the good intended or aimed at. Or, we do not know the good at which we have aimed until we have expressed it in action.

249. The attempt to get a good guaranteed before action is a moral fallacy in

hedonism, and in man's ordinary consciousness. The feeling that one ought not to act until he can see that good is guaranteed hampers action. The element of faith or spontaneity cannot be eliminated. Part of the condition of determining whether the act is good or not is in the act itself. The new situation is a standpoint from which to judge previous situations.

250. The reflection back upon the former conditions gives rise to the category of right and wrong. To say that past civilizations were bad is to judge the past conditions by the standard which is the outcome of the intervening experience. The past acts were bad because they could not be organized into the present self.

251. But it is not true that the people who did the acts were wicked. To say that they were wicked because they did what would be wrong for us is Pharisaism. A false hypothesis rightly followed without prejudice tends to correct itself. So a false ideal followed without prejudice tends to correct itself. A good man frequently follows bad ends, but we call him good if he follows it unreservedly because he will come out right in the end. The person who takes advantage of the new situation reconstructs his ideal. It is never possible to realize a bad ideal because the conditions do not permit it.

252. Method is more important than end because the right method will tend to correct a wrong law. The normal thing is to redefine the ideal. Yet some persons never identify themselves with their actions; they fail to identify the self as agent with the self as organic experience, and blame external conditions. As a matter of description, a good man is any man who identifies himself with the result and reconstructs his ideal. The bad person is any person who refuses to thus identify himself with his activity. Moral standards are largely class standards; and unless we make this distinction we must identify goodness with [a person's] acceptance of class standards rather than judge [him] by the helping on of progress by utilizing experience.

253. Why there should be these two kinds of people cannot be answered in a general way. [In] particular cases, [we] may allow of reasons from [an] absolute knowledge of the individual. The only answer in principle is the fact that we are social beings. If an individual lived alone in the world this distinction could not have arisen. Individuality implies differentiation. One person gets to a given goal sooner than another. If this new experience did not have a social content it could not be said that some did and some did not get at the new experience. Because a person's aims must always be social, because the ideal always affects others, there is ground for this mixing up. One does not identify himself with the consequences of his action, but another is a factor in his action. The latter sees that he cannot change these circumstances which affect him unless he can change the first person's motive. Therefore he says it was a wrong act.

Then he brings that consciously to his attention, which brings conflicting elements into his experience. The first man must then do something with these conflicting elements as facts.

254. One can refuse to recognize the impersonal elements of his experience (as pain), but its impersonal elements will carry their reaction further and force upon him the question of whether he will recognize these elements. Consciousness of wrong comes about through reflection into the intuition of a situation created by an act. The act itself is one interpretation.

255. In simple terms, experience brings light with it. That illumination throws light on the old motive and his badness consists in having chosen this for the good. This dualism in the self constitutes the bad. We are glad in the right and sorry for the wrong. We identify ourselves with the right and so are in it. We refuse to identify ourselves with the wrong, and so contemplate it as away from us.

256. How can we account for a person holding within himself this dual standard, this mixing up? If the individual were a lonesome thing, there would be no ground on which the dualistic standpoint could arise. One's interests always overlap another's. B is an element in A's action. B becomes a conscious agent to force upon A a consciousness of his actions. Because of this actual social unity in conduct, it cannot help having more or less of the dualistic standard. While he has his standard, other people have their standards and force theirs upon him by their actions toward him. It is a conflict between himself as an isolated end and himself as a social end. The way A reacts constitutes the conflict. It is the process of reflecting that constitutes the egoism or altruism, not anything in his constitution.

257. There are two ways in which A will tend to recognize these: his lines of operation. First, there are A's natural inherited tendencies. He has a common social factor in him, physically so to speak. He is a particular differentiation of the life process. He has inherited social instincts. Taken historically, the individual is most sunken [i.e., immersed] in the tribe in the earliest times. Individuality is of late historical growth. It is not, as Rousseau held, individual first and society later. There is instinctive law for the social nature.

258. Then [second] there is the more reflective side. B brings pressure to bear on A. Society, commerce, are pulls which B has on A. Thus, there is the outgoing of his own instinctive nature, and this through demands made by others. A can no more help recognizing these ends than he can help recognizing the ends B calls his own. Now having accounted for him as a social being, we have to go to B and take his side of the case. B stands for all social influences working on A. B tells A he is wrong in doing a certain thing.

259. Now what is B's responsibility and the nature of his act in bringing home

the consciousness of wrong doing to another? A could identify himself with private or common ends. Does not the same thing occur in B, in bringing this to A's consciousness? He can get as far outside of A as possible or he can identify himself with A.

260. A recognition that the selection is organic, mutual, common, and just as much A's end as his own, is one possibility. Thus,[34] if he stands outside of A, B sets up ends just as private as A has, and a conflict between ends results. The empirical correlate of that is what we might call fixed condemnation, i.e., judging [by] ourselves, without trying to bring the individual to the consciousness of the act.

261. Here is a class in society that condemns liquor selling. Is there any moral responsibility in that judgment? The ultimate moral responsibility is the way the condemnation is made. If a class stands off and judges another without recognizing its own moral responsibility, it does wrong. The conditions which give rise to liquor selling are just as much due to one as the other. The one class can not get outside and condemn the other, but must get inside and condemn itself as well, in so far as it is responsible.

262. The effort to change conditions is the only moral judgment. The external condemnation is but self-congratulation. This is the teaching of Christ. The individual is responsible for the ills of society. A's wrong doing is the result of conditions, not because he has recognized the good and then said he would do the wrong.

263. Why then is not all morality and responsibility destroyed? It would be if man were not a social being. It would be if B did not have a wider view to give to A. Because this is not freedom in one sense, do we have responsibility? If A had done wrong of his own choice and by himself, B would condemn him as A, a person. But because A is the result of conditions, B's responsibility becomes deepened to bring a change of conditions to A's consciousness.[35]

264. At times, the simple condemnation will bring one to consciousness of wrong. Then that is right. A great deal of evil goes along in the world simply because it is not condemned, is not named. The very naming of a course of action makes the individual see that he does not want to identify himself with it, and so he changes his action. It is B's responsibility to interpret A's line of action to him.

265. This is the legitimate outcome of Christ's statement, "Judge not." Intellectually, one must judge, must find what the state of things is. In another sense "Judge not" is a moral point. Having sized up the situation, in what form is the intellectual judgment to work itself out? B cannot stand off from A and say he is wrong. Whatever objection could be made to this theory, it could not be that it lowered the responsibility. Judging is only allowable when it is necessary to aid one in acting.

[Chapter 13.] The Nature of the Categories of Responsibility

266. The categories of responsibility and freedom belong to the third stage of the judgment. They express the quality or value of the completed judgment. They do not express the tension. The two are logically correlative. Any system may be considered from the side of organism or of organs. From the standpoint of the former it is freedom; from that of functioning of organs in the organism, it is responsibility. In other terms, if we take the act which is the completed judgment considered as the unity of the self or organization of the situation, freedom comes into play; if we consider the factors which enter into that organization, the category of responsibility comes into play.

267. No fact has any claim to set itself up as an isolated fact; it is open to new discoveries. The new truth transforms or absorbs what has gone before. The conclusion of a syllogism is never drawn from the premises, except psychologically. The conclusion is the premises organized. Obviously, in inductive reasoning, the facts are tentative until the generalization is gotten. The more we develop the theory, e.g., evolution, the more the facts assume new aspects for us. The premises are restated and transformed in the new truth we call the conclusion. Therefore, they can never be isolated, but must always be held open to the transformation.

268. The category of responsibility simply expresses the fact that every activity is an organic part of a whole. Psychologically and morally, every act and impulse that has gone into the completed activity has surrendered its individuality to the organic completed whole. Every member is then responsible to the system. Every act is related organically to other acts. It is, psychologically, a coordination. From the fact that it is a system, it means freedom.

269. In what sense can it be said that a man is responsible? There is general confusion between responsibility *for* an act and responsibility *in* an act. Responsibility for an act means that a person must stand [up for] the consequences of his acts. There is then no doubt about his responsibility. A blind man is thus responsible for his blindness because he has got to recognize it as an organic element in his activities. One has to take the consequences because it is a part of himself. This is simply recognition that any particular act is a part of the whole self. The responsibility must be recognized either positively or negatively. The only sense in which it is true that a man is not responsible for his blindness is that he did not cause it.

270. Is this category of responsibility identical with the category of causation?

Either responsibility means being an element in an organic whole or it means causation. This causation category makes a separation in the self. Supposing the self did not cause the blindness. This implies that the self and the blindness are the same thing. The same is true of the self and the tendency to steal. Is not such a trait a part of the self? Then the category of causation has no application here.

271. When people in society hold each other responsible for certain acts, what do they mean by it? What does liability mean? Compare O. W. Holmes, Jr., *Common Law*.[36] The criterion is the man's actual or presumed ability to foresee the consequences of his act. The whole matter is thrown back on his ability to foresee, not on causation. If rubbish were thrown from a roof and injured a man in the back yard which he ought not to be in, the man on the roof would not be liable. If the same thing [i.e., one man injures another] happened on the street he would be held liable. If the insane man is excused, it is not because there was more causation in his act than in any other act, but because he was not able to relate his act to the consequences, to relate the impulses on which he acted to his other impulses. The same is true of children on account of immaturity that is true of others on account of abnormality.

272. It falls back on our ability to analyze for ourselves the state of mind in which the person was when he did the act. Psychological insight is not yet so far advanced but that we have to leave a certain margin for the individual. It is not necessary to prove that a man on the roof thought that someone would be passing in the street. It is only necessary to prove what the ordinary man must direct [his] attention to, so long as there shall be any society. If he does not come up to that he is held responsible.

273. There has thus been a conflict between the practical actions of man in society and this category of causation. There are conditions, in the past, of any man's past, which would explain and account for his actions at any time. It is absurd that anything in the past can cause anything in the present, in any physical sense. Logical determination is but explanation, and cannot be transferred into physical causation. It is but the recognition of the organic relations of the whole. All men are responsible *for* their acts. Only the good man is responsible *in* his act.

274. These ideas come together when each is analyzed: (1) analysis of judgment, (2) idea of evolution, (3) idea of freedom. The complete judgment is the idea of evolution and that is the idea of freedom. The judgment on the scientific side is: old is new; identity is difference; real is ideal; existence is meaning; analysis is synthetic.

275. Every new judgment that is not tautological takes such a shape. The contradiction arises because it is not seen that the intellectual judgment is to pass

over into new activities. The new activity or situation into which the judgment passes gives us the process of evolution. The scientific judgment, in defining the past, must evolve a new value. Then it is not simply a statement that one thing is another thing. It is the statement of the old facts in a new light.

276. The old in a new light is evolution: a quantitative readjustment. Evolution gets into difficulty when it is attempted to identify the real with a given time. The formula is simply incomplete, and when the formula is completed there is no evolution, e.g., Spencer's "homogeneous" is not satisfactory because there is always a change going on. To define that change means to have a certain limit or purpose in view. That direction in which the movement is going constitutes the ideal element. Hence "real is ideal" is but statement of the idea of evolution.

277. The "latter potentially involved in the earlier" means, not that the potential is a physical thing, but it expresses the ideal element: that the movement is directed toward an end.

278. The conflict in science today arises from the materialistic or psychological ideas. Psychology tends to reduce everything to groups of sensations. Thus, on the scientific side, we get materialism or idealism, according as we start from the material or psychological point.

279. Is there a point of view in science which both of these represent in a one-sided way? On one side science seems to have been permitted to start with physical and adding psychical; on the other to the opposite method.[37] Each of these positions can be equally validated from its own standpoint. This indicates that a false abstraction has been made and the whole has not been recognized.

280. The complete judgment worked out gives the idea of evolution. This is the idea of freedom. If the whole thing is moving, no detail can be fixed unless isolated. And isolation would break up evolution. Every condition is always subject to modification through its dynamic relations to the other parts of the environment.

281. The side of function is always more important than the side of structure. Immediately, the structure will determine the function, but in the long run the function will readjust the structure on the biological side. Environment is (determines) the organ. Spencer is inconsistent in stating in one place that the tongue is made sensitive by constant rubbing against the teeth, etc., and in another that function determines the structure. Function changes both environment and organs, and thus a new function arises. This is freedom. If either the environment or organ is isolated you have either predeterminism or indeterminism. From the above point of view you get determinism, the organ and environment both going back to the definiteness of the function.

Notes

1. In the autobiographical essay, "From Absolutism to Experimentalism" (1930), Dewey speaks approvingly of Auguste Comte's "idea of a synthesis of science that should be a regulative method of an organized social life" (*LW*, 5:154).

2. Perhaps "definite and specific case."

3. This addition is speculative, but Dewey does assert in "The Influence of Darwinism on Philosophy" (1909) that "the conviction persists—though history shows it to be a hallucination—that all the questions that the human mind has asked are questions that can be answered in terms of the alternatives that the questions themselves present" (*MW*, 4:14). Dewey's overall approach in these lectures is to change the question by developing a new account of inquiry.

4. Possibly "our mind."

5. Possibly "won completed experience."

6. According to William James, the "psychologist's fallacy" is "the great snare of the psychologist . . . the confusion of his own standpoint with that of the mental fact about which he is making his report." See Volume 1 of his *Psychology* (New York: Henry Holt, 1990), pp. 196–97. Dewey interprets this to mean that we, as outside psychologists, have a tendency to read into the early stages of a development that which can only be true of the later stages. We do this because we are more interested in the outcome than the process. See Dewey's 1898 "Lectures on Psychological Ethics," *LPPE*, p. 25.

7. In Dewey's "Introduction to Philosophy: Syllabus of Course 5" (1892), the "syncrete" or "internal unity" is one of the subjective categories (*EW*, 3:223).

8. Dewey asserts in his 1892 "Introduction to Philosophy: Syllabus of Course 5": "There are three philosophic sciences, corresponding to three ways in which the individual, or organized action may be regarded. These are Logic, Aesthetic and Ethic" (*EW*, 3:230). The Syllabus concludes with the statement, "Ethic unites the two sides distinguished in logic and aesthetic. It deals with the practical situation; the organized action" (235). These are the only remarks on ethics in the Syllabus, and it is plausible that the remainder of this course is an attempt to develop them further.

9. This paragraph should be taken in conjunction with the assertion in §189 that a person who applies the concept of justice should first get "a mastery of the actual facts to discuss what the actual movement of these facts is."

10. Presumably a reference to Plato and Aristotle in the paragraph above. But Dewey could have said "the universals."

11. The typescript is obscure here.

12. Apparently the reference is to Josiah Royce, *The Spirit of Modern Philosophy* (Boston: Houghton, Mifflin, 1892), mentioned previously in §55.

13. Apparently, the "reflex" refers to the activity of thinking about these conflicting views. In contemporary psychology, the so-called "reflex arc" refers to the activity of thought.

14. Actually refers to "The Chaos in Modern Training" (1894), *EW* 4:106–18.

15. The concept of an "objectified unity" apart from "a unity of life" is puzzling at first. But see Dewey's rejection of the dualism of "the world" and "psychical activity" in §120 of these lectures. There is a discussion of the objectivity of the moral ideal in Dewey's 1900 "Lectures on the Logic of Ethics," *LE*, pp. 63–67, which begins with the assertion that "it is obvious that the ideal cannot be considered objective if the object is identified with anything having an independent external existence . . . in the metaphysical and moral make-up of things . . ." (63). Further, "the ideal is not external to experience as a whole." Dewey's own conception of objectivity as worked out in these pages is related to control in the process of experience. So, then an "objectified unity" is a unity apart from experience, separated from human experience. For an early version of this view associated with Hegel, see "The Present Position of Logical Theory" (1891), *EW*, 3:136–37. For a later version of Dewey's concept of objectivity, see his reply to Philip Blair Rice, in "Valuation Judgments and Immediate Quality," and "Further as to Valuation as Judgment" (1943), *LW*, 15:63–83.

16. That is, the psychological and social sides of experience are two aspects of the same experience as it goes through these stages.

17. A parabola is a conic section, the intersection of a cone with a plane parallel to its side. An hyperbola is a curve formed by action of a right circular cone when the cutting plane makes a greater angle with the base than the cone's side makes.

18. In the Political Ethics lectures to follow, Dewey asserts that "the moral process is never the mere assertion of the idea as such, but is the use of the ideal to manipulate the conditions" (§111).

19. For this view, see *The Study of Ethics*, *EW*, 4:259–60. On this point, Dewey owes a good deal to Samuel Alexander. See the latter's "Natural Selection in Morals," *International Journal of Ethics* 2, no. 4 (July 1892): 409–39. See also Dewey's 1901 "Lectures on Psychological Ethics," *LE*, pp. 231–35, for some examples of ordinary persons working out ideals.

20. For more detail on Dewey's interpretation of the Greek and the "later theory" or Christianity, see the "Introduction to Philosophy, Syllabus of Course 5," *EW*, 3:224–25; see also the 1898 "Lectures on Psychological Ethics," *LPPE*, pp. 11–14.

21. Why not say "the working out of it" instead of the awkward expression "working of it out"? The former suggests there is a pre-existing "it" to be worked out, while Dewey presumably wants to emphasize the dynamic, reconstructive activity of "working out the it."

22. Dewey appears to be saying that there is no need to employ the notion of the actual unless there is conflict, and hence a need to re-affirm, the resources at our command.

23. Or "moral nature." The word 'motive' appears to have been stricken over 'nature' in the typescript.

24. "Moral Theory and Practice" (1891), *EW*, 3:93–109.

25. Herbert Spencer, "Relative and Absolute Ethics," chap. 13 in *The Data of Ethics* (New York: P. F. Collier and Son, 1900), pp. 299–325. The first edition of this work appeared in 1879.

26. *Outlines of a Critical Theory of Ethics* (1891), *EW*, 3:239–388.

27. The word 'perfectionism' is written over, hedonism, in the typescript.

28. See Dewey's "Green's Theory of the Moral Motive" (1892), *EW*, 3:155–73; see also his "Self-Realization as the Moral Ideal" (1893), *EW*, 4:42–53.

29. Quotations added by the editor.

30. Harald Høffding, "The Principle of Welfare," *The Monist* 1 (July 1891): 525–51.

31. T. H. Green, "The Greek and the Modern Conceptions of Virtue," chap. 5 in bk. 3 of *Prolegomena to Ethics*, 2nd ed. (Oxford: The Clarendon Press, 1884).

32. mine and yours.

33. See James Martineau, vol. 2 of *Types of Ethical Theory*, 3rd ed. (Oxford: The Clarendon Press, 1889), chaps. 5, 6.

34. The "thus" here is not used to confirm the affirmation in the previous sentence, but to restate the difficulty regarding how to deal with conflicting ends.

35. Perhaps the term 'situation' would be clearer than 'conditions' in these passages. The required "change of conditions," or change in the situation, is neither inner nor outer, by the individual nor by society; rather it is a change in the functioning elements in the situation needed to restore a mutually acceptable relationship. B has a "wider view" to give to A, but it is not some allegedly superior moral standpoint which B uses to condemn A. It is a knowledge of the change in conditions needed to restore a satisfactory relationship.

36. For Holmes's discussion of this aspect of liability, see Oliver Wendell Holmes Jr., *The Common Law* (Boston: Little, Brown, 1881), pp. 53–62.

37. The materialist scientist starts with the physical and has to explain the psychical. The idealist starts with the psychical and has to explain the physical.

Part Two
Lectures on Political Ethics
Spring Quarter 1896

Editor's Introduction to
the Lectures on Political Ethics

The Significance of the Lectures

The subject matter of the "Lectures on Political Ethics" is the separate and antagonistic spheres of academic and intellectual inquiry commonly designated as Politics, Economics, and Ethics. As we go on to read them over one hundred years after they were delivered, our concern will most likely be as specialists in Dewey's thought. As in the "Lectures on the Logic of Ethics," the issues raised here are abstract and seemingly divorced from present day concerns. As contemporary students of ethics, our immediate concern is likely to be about what ought to be done about such matters as the problems of crime and the decline of education in our inner cities, what would be the proper moral response to the assertion that the federal government is intrusive and inefficient, or how to go about developing laws and policies concerning active, voluntary euthanasia and physician assisted suicide, and so on. Our task as scholars is to formulate a moral answer to these difficulties, but what happens next is out of our hands. Whether or not our moral recommendations will be implemented is a matter for the political theorists, who interpret practical politics. It is also a separate question whether the corporations that constitute the economic process will work for, or at least tolerate, the bringing of our moral recommendations into reality. Economic theory is called upon to explain the actions of entrepreneurs. As moral philosophers, it is not our business to concern ourselves with such economic matters.

The scenario just set forth suggests how discussion about specific matters of moral concern can get turned around. Our initial interest is often practical: to find a working moral solution as to what ought to be done. But, lacking any account of the manner in which a proposed "working moral solution" is to become actualized within the existing political and economic processes, our self-professed practical concern is abandoned. Moral inquiry now becomes "theory," with its own modes of inquiry and thought. Qua theory, inquirers create an approach to its unique subject matter, method, rules of success and failure. This approach is sustained independently of whether anyone does or does not "follow" the recommendations made in its name. Meanwhile, practical political activity and practical economic activity deal with separate subject matters. Politics is about power. Economics is about the activities of rational, self-interested humans, both as entrepreneurs and as consumers.

There is a striking confirmation of this state of affairs in a recent book, *The Crisis of Vision in Modern Economic Thought*. The authors, Robert Heilbroner and William Milberg, are searching for a new "classical situation" or widely accepted consensus in economic theory that will respond to the social difficulties of our own day. But theoretical economists have cut themselves off from any effort to gain political influence, while ordinary business life is governed in practice by the quest for indefinite capital accumulation. The authors, *qua* economists, can offer no rational basis for moral reform with regard to the growing poverty of the lower income segment of the population or to global environmental destruction. From their point of view, moral considerations are "pre-analytic." Nor do the authors do anything to dispel the widely accepted view that politics, as reflected in the "public sector" of the economy, "speaks with a voice that has no presumed internal rationality, and from a past too often associated with various forms of oppression."[1]

So Dewey's concern about the interrelation of Politics, Economics, and Ethics is of current interest. If the scenario set forth by the academic inquirers is correct, our social life, that is, our activities, relationships, and interactions with others, seems to be divided against itself. As economic persons, we are self-interested but without political power. As political persons we seek this power, or at least have an influence on it. Yet, as ethical persons we denounce self-interest and the quest for power apart from whatever role we are playing in the economic and political process.

Is this state of affairs a reflection of the activities of individuals participating in the social process, or does it indicate a serious flaw in our theoretical categories? These lectures take the latter position. They are a continuation of Dewey's effort to get behind distinctions that are made in the course of inquiry and then taken to indicate dualisms. In political inquiry, the theory of sovereignty or supreme political power leads to a dualism between the expression of power and morality as expression of the moral will. The development of economic theory adds the third factor of individuals' fixed self-interest as what is essential to the economic side of life. In sum, political power is separated from the expression of morality through the will, and economic self-interest is separated from both the quest for political power and morality.

The lectures take on these separations by extending the logic of inquiry developed in the "Lectures on the Logic of Ethics."[2] In Hegelian language, they carry the inquiry from its most abstract phase, wherein the common features of all judgments take the subject-copula-predicate form, to the concrete life of the particular individual as it takes place in social settings and political institutions. In Dewey's language, this social aspect of the life process completes the organic circuit that constitutes experience, by providing the ongoing stimuli that allow for the continuity of experience as well as its occasional difficulties.

In addition, these lectures unlock significant logical barriers that stand in the way of our understanding Dewey's mature theory of social inquiry. To show this we need to put forth the hypothesis that Dewey's account of inquiry in general, and social inquiry in particular, constitutes a progressive, developing continuum of investigation, from the earliest years to the latest. A continuum is commonly defined as a whole, no part of which can be distinguished from neighboring parts except by arbitrary division. If we apply this definition to Dewey's account of social inquiry, it suggests that, although we must start at some "arbitrary part" in the continuum if we are to understand the "whole," we must also understand the continuum itself, because it *is* the whole. While the latter task cannot be undertaken in a brief introduction, we can show how the understanding of a later "part" in the continuum, in particular Dewey's account of social inquiry in his 1938 volume, *Logic: The Theory of Inquiry*, can benefit from the earlier part set forth in these lectures.

We find in chapter 24 of the *Logic* that serious social troubles tend to be interpreted in moral terms: ". . . the presence of *practical* difficulties should operate, as within physical inquiry itself, as an intellectual stimulus and challenge to further application." "Social conflicts and confusions exist in fact before problems for inquiry exist."[3] Then,

> problems, if they satisfy the conditions of scientific method, (1) grow out of actual social tensions, needs, "troubles"; (2) have their subject-matter determined by the conditions that are material means of bringing about a unified situation, and (3) be related to some hypothesis, which is a plan and policy for existential resolution of the conflicting social situation.[4]

The task involves "the work of analytic discrimination, which is necessary to convert a problematic situation into a set of conditions forming a definite problem." This demands "*intellectual* formulation of conditions; and such a formulation demands in turn complete abstraction from the qualities of sin and righteousness, of vicious and virtuous motives, that are so readily attributed to individuals, groups, classes, nations." This "approach to human problems in terms of moral blame and moral approbation, of wickedness or righteousness, is probably the greatest single obstacle now existing to development of competent methods in the field of social subject matter."[5]

But how can we conduct social inquiry on a moral basis without setting forth what is righteous and what is wicked? We need a new theory of "logical conceptions" and "logical conditions." "The ultimate ground of every valid proposition and warranted judgment consists in some existential reconstruction ultimately effected."[6]

> The special lesson which the logic of the methods of physical inquiry has to teach social inquiry is . . . that social inquiry, *as inquiry*, involves the necessity of operations which existentially modify actual conditions that, as they exist, are the occasions of genuine inquiry and that provide its subject-matter. . . . this lesson is the logical import of the experimental method.[7]

Social inquiry reflects the "experiential continuum and the continuity of inquiry." In the long run, it reflects "the self-developing and self-correcting nature of scientific inquiry."[8]

What do Dewey's remarks imply? Where do they lead us? In sum, supposing we accept them, what are we supposed to do next? As stated earlier, the economic theorist will regard social activity as governed by self-interest, and the political theorist will say that the issue is power. The relationship between the quest for power that governs political life and the self-interest that governs economic life is not clear. Meanwhile, the moral theorist informs everyone that they should ignore power and self-interest, and instead act morally. But once we grant that power and self-interest are the principle motivating forces in social life, it appears that morality has no means to carry out its goals.

If we grant the conclusions of these varieties of theory, Dewey's appeal to "scientific inquiry" in matters of social concern will not be taken up as a starting point for further, more specific inquiries. For it will be alleged that any proposed scientific activity can only serve the activities pursued by the three antagonistic disciplines of Politics, Economics, and Ethics. It does not come first. So then, how does philosophy as "having its distinctive position amongst various modes of criticism in its generality"[9] deal with this problem? How can we develop a scientific treatment of social inquiry that will deal with "the deepest problem of modern life" and restore the "integration" of "man's beliefs about the world in which he lives" as they are investigated by the scientist, as well as "the values and purposes that should direct his conduct"?[10] How do we connect the means generated through scientific and technological inquiry with proposed human ends?

Reconstruction of the Theory of Sovereignty

The 1895 "Lectures on the Logic of Ethics" have given a preliminary answer to these questions. The distinction between the scientific judgment and the moral judgment is made in order to locate and deal with the problematic. The two judgments share in the fact that they are responses to the problem and reflect our effort to control experience. To the extent that human problems are responses that require hypotheses to deal with them, they are *already* scientific problems. It is not the case that we *first* have a human problem and *then*, at some later point, introject scientific inquiry in order to deal with it. The starting point of all inquiry is scientific in the sense that it requires an hypothesis that will, when applied and successfully confirmed through our experience, resolve the problem.

How, though, are we to apply this general approach to inquiry to social problems? As we have seen, the immediate barrier to such inquiry is the separation between Politics, Ethics, and Economics. The notion of inquiry as a response to the problematic "cuts across" this barrier so that these apparently separate inquiries can be regarded as distinctions made in this response. How does Dewey work this out?

The argument attempts to deal with the problem set at the end of Dewey's March 1894 article, "Austin's Theory of Sovereignty."[11]

> The practical, as well as the theoretical problem of sovereignty, may fairly be said to be this: To unite the three elements . . . force, or effectiveness [Politics]; universality, or reference to interests and activities of society as a whole [Ethics]; and determinateness, or specific modes of operations—definite organs of expression [Economics].

In Dewey's proposed reconstruction,

> (1) The economic phase is a question of mechanism or machinery by which individuals reciprocally stimulate and control each other. When we ask how an individual stimulates and controls, we have a question of economics. (2) If we ask concerning the structure of the organism through which this reciprocal relation and response is exercised, and through which the conscious values are mediated, we have the political question. (3) The ethical question is a question of ends. Economics is a question of means. Politics is a question of the adjustment of the two, or the technique. Ethics gives the idea of freedom, that is, the amount of value of social activities which is absorbed. On the side of economics it is demands. On the side of Politics it is the assumed rights of the individual and the organ; it is goods, powers, claims.

> On the side of readjustment, Ethics gives us responsibility, Economics gives us supply, and Politics obligations. The organization of social consciousness is to maintain the equilibrium between freedom and responsibility, demand and supply, rights and obligations. (§75, 76)

In other words, if we start with problematic situations that arise within our social life, the three disciplines reflect distinctions made within it for the purpose of dealing with the problem, not separate areas of inquiry.

How does Dewey arrive at this conclusion? The classic problem of political sovereignty is about the location of supreme political power as the basis for social control. The nineteenth-century political and legal theorist, John Austin, takes the view that the political sovereign is determinate, yet he cannot explain how this determinate power actually functions to get everyone to obey. By contrast, Rousseau holds there is a general will, but he cannot account for its ongoing organs of expression. Thus, Dewey asks,

> Now do these two exhaust the alternatives? This old question again between the universal and the particular, between organism and its various organs! The dilemma is a self-made one, not arising in the nature of the case, but in setting the particular over against the whole. (§98)

The difficulty here illustrates Dewey's assertion in his 1901 "Lectures on Social Ethics" that "the fundamental ethical problem is the relation of the particular to the universal."[12] The problem is at once theoretical and practical. True, we tend to think of the instrumentalist standpoint as a reconstruction of the evolutionary view that biological organisms produce variations. If so, humans can and do utilize creative intelligence to characterize and resolve their own problems, and all inquiry is particular. Where, then, is there room for consideration of the "whole," which in this case is the overall social process? At any rate, we cannot ignore the whole to the extent that we are participants in it and affected by it.

In his early essay, "The Sentiment of Rationality" (1879), William James compares the person who seeks simplification by showing that "a chaos of facts is the expression of a single underlying fact" with its "sister passion, which in some minds . . . is its rival, . . . the passion for distinguishing, . . . the impulse to be *acquainted* with the parts rather than to comprehend the whole." We are caught between these two tendencies. Hence,

> the unsatisfactoriness of all our speculations. On the one hand, so far as they retain any multiplication in their terms, they fail to get us out of the empirical sand-heap world; on the other, so far as they eliminate multiplicity, the practical man despises their empty barrenness. The most they can say is that the elements of the world are such and such, and that each is identical with itself wherever found.[13]

Once we regard those theorists who favor getting acquainted with the "elements" as pragmatists, then much contemporary theory is, in this sense, pragmatic. For example, the moral philosophers mentioned in the first paragraph of this introduction are concerned about crime and the failure of education. However, they ignore, or at least play down, the scientific or factual aspect of the "whole," while concentrating on the "part" concerned with morality. As practical individuals, they may also play down ethical theory as a comprehensive discipline about the moral life in order to deal with specific, down-to-earth, moral issues that arise within the overall social process and occupy our interest. Meanwhile, the economist ignores the ethical side of the whole and continues to develop a comprehensive theory based upon the assumption of the rational, self-interested entrepreneur and the consumer. Yet, for many economists this theoretical framework is only a backdrop for particular investigations into the movement of prices in a particular marketplace, the effects of mergers upon prices and quality, or forecasts about specific aspects of the economy. Meanwhile, some political theorists take up the all-encompassing theories of Plato, Hobbes, Locke, and Herbert Spencer, while others disdain overall theory and get down to specific issues.

In sum, the abstraction that is required to express the whole process—everything that is happening in a complex contemporary social process—is likely to result in a theory that, in James's words, has only an "empty barrenness" that cannot bear practical fruit. Our alternative is to stick to the specific aspects of the inquiry pursued by James's "practical man". But if the "whole" impinges upon and is relevant to the practical problem, what does the practical person do next? The whole of ethical theory is relevant to particular moral decisions. Likewise, the whole of political theory is relevant to particular political problems, as the whole of economic theory is relevant to particular economic explanations. Further, the subject matters of all these theories constitute a whole that impinges upon the individual making a practical decision. How do we find a way to turn the whole from an obstacle, consisting of these three antagonistic parts, into a means?

Dewey's Location of the Problem

The two problems we have been discussing express different sides of the same coin. The problem concerning the relation of the part to the whole finds expression through the breakdown of the traditional view that political sovereignty can be found in a single location. Rather, sovereignty is found in the specific workings of the entire social process.[14] The disharmony between the parts or particulars that we designate as Ethics, Politics, and Economics, as well as the more specific practical inquiries we conduct in their name, raises the question about the relation of these parts to the whole process or social organism.[15]

The "same coin" is the problematic situation, which functions as an instrumental device to locate the problem.[16] Start with any problematic situation that occurs within the whole social process, and the three inquiries reflect distinctions made within this process in order to deal with it. These distinctions are devices or instruments that are constructed as society passes from the more primitive to the more complex and progressive, and as scientific activity and its technological outgrowths change our lives.[17] These devices reflect our effort to deal with increasingly complex situations as society evolves over the course of human history.

More particularly, the development of morality and of moral control is located within the social process. It is not outside the process, as suggested by Rousseau's theory of the general will that operates apart from the specific, ongoing activities of life. Nor are we to regard these activities as merely *de facto*, and hence as non-moral or immoral. If this view seems strange, impossible, or obviously incorrect, it is perhaps because we have an image or picture of the overall social process and the activities of individuals within it that does not permit us to entertain Dewey's standpoint. We think of morality as above or prior to both individual activity and the activity of groups; we think of power—whether it be the control of one individual over another or of an organization over an individual—as something non-moral or morally neutral. Yet we have seen in our discussion of the "Lectures on the Logic of Ethics" that the moral and the factual are distinctions made in response to the problematic. The notion of a response implies power, control, and thought as integrated with action. What remains to be seen is how this response takes on a moral character.

We will start with the notion of an organic circuit and consider the interaction between the individual and society as the source of social control. The standpoint stated in technical language in these lectures is restated in simpler terms in chapter 4 of *Experience and Education* (1938), with the example of children playing in a baseball game at recess or after school. Dewey points out that "games do not go on haphazardly or by a succession of improvisations," since "without rules there is no game." Further, "if disputes arise there is an umpire to appeal to, or discussion and a kind of arbitration are means to a decision; otherwise the game is broken up and comes to an end." Dewey goes on to point out three "obvious controlling features in such situations."

The first is that the rules are a part of the game. They are not outside of it. No rules, then no game; different rules, then a different game. As long as the game goes on with a reasonable smoothness, the players do not feel that they are submitting to external imposition but that they are playing the game. In the second place an individual may at times feel that a decision isn't fair and he may even get angry. But he is not objecting to a rule but to what he claims is a violation of it, to some one-sided and unfair action. In the third place, the rules, and hence the conduct of the game are fairly standardized. These rules have the sanction of tradition and precedent.

Using this example to illustrate a "general principle," Dewey asserts "In all such cases it is not the will or desire of any one person which establishes order but the moving spirit of the whole group. The control is social, but individuals are parts of a community, not outside of it."[18] This is a concrete example of the standpoint stated abstractly in these lectures.

The self is a "progressive synthesis" within the social process, not a "soul" or "fixed entity" that exists apart from that process. The latter, as studied by Sociology, is not a "bridge on top" of the self, which tries to restrain the action of the individual, but a "genetic unity" that includes the functional relations of the various selves, "a unity out of which the different [social] sciences were differentiated" (§7–8). How then do the "facts" get differentiated into Ethics, Politics, and Economics?

First [we] must have genetic unity or origin; second, [we must have] functional unity on the side to which it points. A new science is not cumulative, but represents a new point of view, and has to reconstruct the categories at the basis of the other sciences. . . . society is either an organism or it is not. If it is, it affects all of these facts of Ethics and Economics; it is not something besides these (§8).

Dewey criticizes E. A. Ross's sociological standpoint because he holds that

man had a soul as a special possession apart from other people. At that time, however, an organic society was not thought of. The notion of an organic society was the outgrowth of the same *Zeitgeist* out of which the new psychology came. If you write of the new society, you must also use the new psychology. (§9)

Specifically, the individual is an organ who can be characterized in terms of functional interactions within the organism as a social process. The individual interacts with other individuals in the organism. Or, as a member of an organization such as the family, at the work place, or in a voluntary organization such as a labor union, an individual interacts with (and sometimes comes in conflict with) members of other organizations. There is no conflict between the individual as such and society as such (§49).

There are problematic situations *within* the overall organic process, not *between* a fixed, ready-made, presumably self-interested individual and some other process taken at large and designated by the term 'society.' If Dewey is correct on this point, the entire focus of inquiry with regard to the "problems of men" is shifted from the search for an outside source of moral control as given by "Ethics" or an account of social control as given by "Politics". Distinctions and differentiations are made, but they are part of the evolutionary process. As we have already seen in the Logic of Ethics lectures, the predicate of a sentence represents the variable factor, not a fixed entity. The quest for differentiation is evolutionary, and it "falls within the sphere of means and ends" (§14).

> An organism is a mass which is concentrated and replaced through the intensification and direction of energy. The whole process of evolution is an integration of matter everywhere. From this point of view a living organism represents a peculiar concentration. What is meant by 'replaced' is plain. It is the idea of a circuit, of coming around again and repairing its own waste by what it does. (§15)

In sum, the respective notions of the evolutionary process and the repairing of waste through the biological organism are continuous with the creative intelligence of the human. There is no ethical factor that is introduced from outside of the evolutionary-organic process.

The notion of a "circuit" leads us to Dewey's unique interpretation of the notions of stimulus and response in restoring continuity to the organism.[19] In his important article, "The Reflex Arc Concept in Psychology," published in 1896 at about the same time these lectures were given, he asserts that

> the stimulus is that phase of the forming co-ordination which represents the conditions which have to be met in order to bring it to a successful issue; the response is that phase of one and the same forming co-ordination which gives the key to meeting these conditions, which serves as instrument in effecting the successful co-ordination.[20]

In the language of these lectures, the stimulus is not an external factor to keep people in line. It is the element in the "forming coordination," the socio-environmental phase of the forming coordination. The response, or active factor in the coordination, is not a fixed self that is struggling to realize itself over against the socio-environmental factor. It is an active, forming, reconstructing self that is seeking to restore continuity through the use of creative intelligence.

> The relative opposition in consciousness between the individual and his associated activity arises when the individual finds it necessary to bring to con-

sciousness his activity, that is, the stimuli to control and the standard of control. The fallacy comes in when this apparent opposition is taken for an absolute opposition, and an historical value for an inherent value. (§45)

The whole question of social organization is a question of organizing stimuli and responses. It is a question on the individual side . . . [about] the stimulation of the individual. On the social side, [the question is] how far are channels of stimuli organized so they react on special stimuli in a way to control as well as re-stimulate it, that is, give the individual activity a definite place in the whole? All mechanisms of society are not so many various things, but modes in which the one question is being worked out; that is, all processes and activities of society fundamentally are to be regarded on the basis of the part they play in constituting this social sensorium. The social sensorium is an organization of stimuli and responses of various individuals in the social group. (§71)

At this point, Dewey's reconstruction of the various dualisms in our methods of inquiry is virtually complete. The "social sensorium" includes all the factors in society that function to stimulate the individual and give him or her a place in the whole. It includes newspapers, as well as the competitive and educative processes.[21]

The dissolution of the separation between politics, economics, and ethics has been accomplished. What remains is to determine the positive role of each of the three phases within the overall social organism.

The Positive Side of the Three Phases

The Overall Social Process

Economics. Dewey's interpretation of the economic phase of the social organism is unique. He ignores the traditional view that it is the fixed self-interest of individual entrepreneurs and customers that drives economic competition.[22] Success is a function of intelligence locating the market for a product, by using information obtained through the social sensorium.

If you have any division of labor, you have to have some principle of division, that is, the activity of each one in the community has got to be controlled by demands made by the community as a whole and by the demands of others. This means there must be a social sensorium. (§150)

The question is how is the relation between supply and demand to be maintained? Spencer assumes that competition will do it. The reason the lungs, heart, etc. don't get all [i.e., everything] for themselves, respectively, is because there is the nervous system which acts as umpire. That is the reason there is working equilibrium established. Why doesn't man make too many plows, or too few, for the community? Because of the social sensorium, that is, the individual controls his manufacture by feeling the demand of [the] community. (§151)

The controlling power in the distribution of the industrial system will always be the existing social sensorium. (§152)[23]

In sum, the success of competition cannot be explained by the operation of fixed self-interest.

Politics. On the political side of the social process there is no single sovereign. Customs guide ordinary activity, and eventually custom becomes solidified into law. As suggested by the example of baseball in *Experience and Education,* government plays the role of umpire.

Every institution is habit and therefore sovereignty, as a whole, is defined in law. . . . law is the functional direction of habit. This law is determined on one side in right, that is, stimuli involved in [the] exercise of habit; and on the other side in obligations, which are inhibitions and control in the operation of habit. (§84)

The fallacy of explaining sovereignty as force *per se* arises there. All will is forceful. Will means the struggle to realize one's own ideals. As society developed, it was found advisable to regulate this force. . . . One organ is differentiated to do the controlling work for the sake of economy, for example, an umpire in a game. (§86)

It is helpful at this point to bring up Dewey's contrast between "primitive times" and the customary society on one hand, and the progressive society on the other.[24] In the primitive, or customary, society, the individual reflects his or her social status and is without individual rights (§53), and "law is simply the crystallization of custom" (§97). "Most of the difficulties will be solved on the basis of custom," as in the Roman Empire (§100). What about the progressive society, or society in which the self is a "progressive synthesis" (§7), where individual social consciousness "marks the nodal point in social evolution"? (§33). "He represents the progressive variation of the social consciousness" (§33). Why is there a demand for such variation? Because "there are too many customs not adapted to each other and they must conflict" (§101). Moreover, "in every progressive society conflict of rights must arise. . . . In stationary society there need be no conflict theoretically" (§127).

Ethics. On the ethical side, there are existing rights and duties, and there is a place for the role of intelligence in reconstructing the moral life.

A system of rights and duties is the organization by which members of the social organism reciprocally stimulate and control each other's actions. It is impossible in this to separate the idea and the mechanism side. One individual can't stimulate another individual. There must be some medium of interaction. (§124)

The ethical question is the question of the extent and manner in which the various activities are translated over into conscious values. It is a question not of a particular mechanism in which this control goes on, or a structure in which the mechanism is centered, but of how far and in what way the activities come to consciousness, and in what way they are present as conscious values. . . . There are no moral values except in consciousness, so to take any value as value is to raise the ethical question. (§73, 74)

The reference to "how far and in what way activities come to consciousness" uses idealist language to express the activity of using intelligence to formulate hypotheses in order to deal with the morally problematic. Much of Dewey's moral philosophy that followed these lectures was devoted to working out an account of this process.

The Task of Reconstruction

Returning to such problems as crime and education, the alleged intrusiveness of the federal government, and the effort to formulate a policy about active euthanasia, these are representative of the issues that concern us now. What might Dewey have to say about them? In terms of his "five logically distinct steps" in thinking discussed in the "Editor's Introduction to the Logic of Ethics" in this volume, Dewey would recognize them as "felt difficulties," but not, initially at least, as moral problems. Each human being, regarded as a member in various groups and associations, already has a economic, political, and moral aspect. The problems, after all, are about crime and the failure of education, about a federal government that seems remote to many people, and about the need to deal with death in cases where there is severe pain. Existing economic, political, and moral aspects of life are often obstacles to the problem, as well as the only available material for its resolution. Each aspect is a condition of the problem that needs to be located, and one or more of these conditions needs to be reconstructed. Then, to revert to the account given previously from Dewey's 1938 *Logic*, the proposed reconstruction takes the form of an hypothesis that, once it is tried out, will resolve the problem. The task of intelligence is to develop these hypotheses.

This outline provides the general setting for Dewey's social thought in 1896 and can be used as a device for explaining his later social thought. The reader of these lectures will likely reject Dewey's contention in §57 of the lectures that the disintegration brought about by social conflict is only "the negative side

of the formation of a more comprehensive unity." The assertion seems too op-
timistic, and perhaps even "Hegelian" in the sense that it vaguely suggests that
this unity is somehow already worked out. He or she may also question the
standpoint reflected in the lectures and worked out in much more detail in the
1898 "Lectures on Political Ethics" and the 1901 "Lectures on Social Ethics"—
that social conflict takes place primarily between social functions (for example,
labor and management) rather than between the individual and the state.
Dewey's view that government is a social organ for the resolution of these conflicts may seem too simplistic. Perhaps, as he argued later in *The Public and its
Problems* (1927, *LW*, vol. 2), there is a need to form new publics to deal with new
problems. Perhaps the current situation calls for new and as yet unforeseen reconstructions of our social life.

Conclusion: Dewey's Account of the Logic of Progress

Faith in human progress was one of the staples of nineteenth-century political
and social discussion. Today we are not so sure. Discussion about the concept
of progress can not, by itself, tell us whether we are progressing. However, it is
significant because our conception of progress regulates the specific inquiries
we pursue in the name of progress.[25] Dewey's account of progress can be called
response-oriented, where friction or tension initiates inquiry, the conditions of
action are the controlling factor in the inquiry, and progress consists in gener-
ating an effective response. This contrasts with the traditional *external goal-oriented* account of progress, whereby the task of inquiry is to justify goals that are
external to the friction generated in a particular problematic situation. In this
latter case, the justified goal becomes a standard of progress or the lack of
progress, as we either approach it or fall away from it.

Dewey's account of progress is generated within his theory of inquiry as it
is worked out in the Logic of Ethics lectures, but it is employed in the "Lectures
on Political Ethics." He apparently became interested in the theory of progress
in the early 1890s, probably due to the influence of Samuel Alexander's *Moral
Order and Progress* (1889).[26] In *The Study of Ethics: A Syllabus* (1894), Dewey criticizes "theories of abstract ideals," or ideals that set a fixed standard external to
experience. "No basis is afforded for the development of moral ideals—for positive moral progress. The ideal is there once for all and it is only a question of
greater or less distance from it."[27] The earliest statement of Dewey's alternative
theory of progress is contained in a set of lecture notes from an 1893 Political
Philosophy course at the University of Michigan.

The theory of progress is more difficult than the theory of order. The material for the latter is pretty well worked out in law. Here there are no defined laws.

Progress equals consciousness of progress. It *is* consciousness! It is in there and nowhere else. Other changes are simply redistribution. There is no distribution of higher and lower except in consciousness. Except in consciousness there is no reason why complexity is higher than simplicity, protoplasm than rock. Value means consciousness. Conclusions that follow:

1. There is no such thing as absolute progress, from a fixed beginning to a fixed end.

2. In discussing the worth of any historical fact or institution we must inquire not what it was in itself but what it did in affecting consciousness. It is relative to the particular past and future considered. A thing is lower when we treat it as a means or a part, higher when we consider it as an end or a whole. So [it is a matter of] better and worse. Except comparatively, a thing is what it is. Taken by itself each age is no better or worse than any other: no different sum total of happiness. Any solution of old problems makes new ones.

3. We cannot compare good and, say, better, best. The good and the best are the same.

4. It is an historical fallacy to consider earlier states as lower in themselves. We first take the previous state as it was and then, putting our present consciousness into it, we call it lower or worse.

5. The future will be higher than the present only in the sense that it will have new ends.[28]

What does Dewey mean by the assertion "Progress equals consciousness of progress"? This statement is repeated in the "Lectures on the Logic of Ethics" as "There is no progress except the consciousness of progress" (§238). Then he adds that

If this is true you must pay the cost of the tension or conflict in order to get the consciousness. . . . If there is no tension between suggested impulses, [so] that we could get everything we want at once, would there be any basis for determining the respective values of these impulses? Could you consciously say that any one of them was good at all? Unless you have some conflict between respective impulses, you cannot compare them at all.

Clearly, then, the new need for progress begins with conflict and seeks to remove the conflict. This leads us back to Dewey's account of goals earlier in the Logic of Ethics lectures.

Goals are just as much local and temporary as standpoints. The concept of 'goal' is also relative, or historical, as well as [a] standing point. The reality is the whole process, the activity which continually produces discrimination and leads on to

> unified experience again. . . . the concept 'goal' is also temporary. There is no
> absolute goal. We constantly create the goal. So, not only are the inner goals rel-
> ative, but the goal "perfection" is also. We continually set up a new goal or end,
> not because of the failure of a previous one, but because of the success in reach-
> ing past goals. (§78)

This account of the concept of a goal may seem like an invitation for the individual to do whatever he or she wants to solve the problem, even if it is at the
expense of others. We will return to this point in a moment, but first let us flesh
out Dewey's conception of progress.

Progress occurs with regard to two contingent points, the occurrence of a difficulty and the proposed ideal that resolves it. The alternative view, as expressed
in many traditional ethical theories, is to set some fixed standard of good or obligation that is external to the situation of the individual. Say, for example, pleasure is alleged to be good; and, following the utilitarian standpoint, our obligation is to maximize the good. Assume pleasure can be conceived of as a kind
of quality of feeling that can be characterized (presumably in units or quantities) independently of the individual who experiences it. Then the individual
can seek more and more pleasure, that is, good. The "absolute right," as Herbert
Spencer holds, is set by "the action that brought pleasure, and pleasure only, to
all concerned" (*Logic of Ethics*, §191). As another example, Kantians and others
hold that there are moral principles that exist in some sense and can be defended
as correct independently of the respective situations of those individuals to
whom they apply. We say, for example, everyone is obligated to follow certain
moral principles. Then progress is measured by the degree to which people approach perfection in the following of these principles.

Dewey's conception of progress as an activity within consciousness or experience is a rejection of this traditional view. As noted earlier in our discussion,
we are at first inclined to question him, because we think his view leads to a fundamental conflict between progress for an individual and progress for everyone
else. But how we interpret this conflict is a function of the conditions of action
as the controlling factor in conduct.

In the "Lectures on Political Ethics," Dewey explains that the conflict between
the good of the individual and the good the society is a phase in the process of
experience, and not a fundamental conflict. So, early in the "Lectures on Political Ethics" he asserts

> At the moment of friction, the organism sets itself up as an individual over
> against the environment. The relative opposition between organism and envi-
> ronment arises when the immediate and the indirect factors do not converge
> without a readjustment of both, that is, when the mediate side itself has to be

readjusted in order to reach the end. The change, which is really a change of the whole is explained always from the standpoint of one [side]. A mediation of the form environment and organism explains a change in the situation. The situati is the whole, viewed from the point of [view of] the environment; functioi ig is the whole from the point of [view of] the organism. (§20)

Ther s a sense in which the remainder of the "Lectures on Political Ethics" is a wc ting out of this point with regard to the social process. So, for example,

V at we have seen so far is that the individual may be considered as a concen-
ted situation. Also that the adapted individual marks one limit in the rhyth-
ic process. The other is that where the situation comes reflexively to con-
iousness as a means to its further development. . . . The fallacy of setting
idividual absolutely over against society is the neglect of the fact that the indi-
ridual, by taking a negative attitude towards past habits, is only the instrument
for social advancement. This makes [for] a most close relation between individual and society. That is, social progress is always precarious except so far as
it becomes a method in the individual's consciousness, abstracted from the content. (§47)

The last sentence sums up the basic point of view put forth in the two sets of lectures in this volume.

Notes

1. Robert Heilbroner and William Milberg, *The Crisis of Vision in Modern Economic Thought* (Cambridge: Cambridge University Press, 1995), pp. 94–95, 113, 126. The authors present a well-argued case for the inadequate response of contemporary economic theory to contemporary moral and political problems.

2. Towards the end of his 1901 "Lectures on Social Ethics," Dewey asserts that his lectures have not been so much on social ethics as on the logic of social ethics (*LE*, p. 431). I believe this holds true for these lectures as well.

3. Quotations in this paragraph are from *LW*, 12:488, 485, 492.

4. *LW*, 12:493.

5. Quotations in this paragraph are from *LW*, 12:487, 488, 489.

6. Quotations in this paragraph are from *LW*, 12:481, 483.

7. *LW*, 12:486–87.

8. *LW*, 12:483.

9. See Dewey, *Experience and Nature, LW*, 1:298.

10. The quotation is from Dewey's *The Quest for Certainty, LW*, 4:104.

11. *EW*, 4:90. Dewey's discussion of sovereignty in the lectures (§80–103) is a reworking of the argument of this article. The discussion, when taken in conjunction with the treatment of sovereignty in the 1898 "Lectures on Political Ethics" (*LPPE*, pp. 408–33),

shows the seminal importance of his criticism of Austin for the development of Dewey's social theory. For an historical analysis of theories of sovereignty, see F. H. Hinsley, *Sovereignty* (New York: Basic Books, 1966).

12. *LE*, p. 328.

13. Quotations in this paragraph are from William James, "The Sentiment of Rationality," reprinted in *Essays in Pragmatism* (New York: Hafner, 1969), pp. 5, 7.

14. For this view see §81–86.

15. In the these lectures, Dewey develops the notion that society is a complex organism, whose functioning parts both contribute to and benefit from the whole (§71)—hence, the explanation for rights and responsibilities (§76). Dewey's attempt to develop a working, dynamic version of the organic theory of society is central to these lectures. His best discussion of the attempt to work out a "dynamic" version of this theory, which explains the positive function of antagonism between the parts, can be found in his 1901 "Lectures on Social Ethics," sections 3–6, *LE*.

16. See the section on "Historical Background" in the Introduction to the "Lectures on the Logic of Ethics" for Dewey's five steps in a complete act of thought, including the location of the problem and the use of the five steps as a device for interpreting the development of Dewey's thought.

17. In Dewey's introduction to the 1948 edition of *Reconstruction in Philosophy*, he criticizes those who think we already have the moral categories to deal with the present situation: " . . . to assume that they are at hand is to assume that intellectual growths which reflect a pre-scientific state of human affairs, concerns, interests and ends are adequate to deal with a human situation which is increasingly and for a very large part the outgrowth of a new science" (*MW*, 12:269).

18. Quotations are from *Experience and Education*, *LW*, 13:32–33. In a discussion of voluntary associations (§86), Dewey asserts that "one organ is differentiated to do the controlling work for the sake of economy, for example, an umpire in a game." He evidently had some interest in sports when he was teaching at the University of Michigan, and perhaps this interest was carried over into his discussion of education in 1938.

19. If we use the expression "restoring continuity within the organism," we suggest that there is somehow an organism outside of the organic process (social process) that needs to have its continuity restored. But the restoration of continuity is carried out within the overall process.

20. *EW*, 5:109.

21. See §147–48, §168–72.

22. For Dewey's criticism of psychological egoism at this stage of his career, see section 2, chapter 6 of his 1898 "Lectures on Psychological Ethics," *LPPE*, pp. 208–18.

23. Dewey gives an expanded account of the economic process in his 1898 "Lectures on Political Ethics," chap. 5 of *LPPE*, pp. 389–407, and his 1901 "Lectures on Social Ethics," sections 8–9 of *LE*, pp. 387–419. In these lectures, he also brings out the importance of science and technology for the evolution of commodities. For more detail on Dewey's economic theory, see the editor's introductions to *Lectures by John Dewey [1915–1916]:*

Moral and Political Philosophy, ed. Warren J. Samuels and Donald F. Koch, in *Research in the History of Economic Thought and Methodology*, Archival Supplement 1 (Greenwich, Connecticut, 1989).

24. The role of a progressive society in the transition from the fixed individual to the "psychological individual," or individual who is capable of self-conscious initiation and variation, is worked out in the Introduction to Dewey's 1898 "Lectures on Psychological Ethics," *LPPE*, pp. 3–34. Roughly speaking, a progressive society is one in which individuals are not bound by custom and in which social conditions encourage individuals to respond to social problems.

25. See the "Lectures on the Logic of Ethics" (§252), where Dewey asserts that "the right method will correct a wrong [moral] law." Instead of identifying goodness with the "acceptance of class standards," we should "judge [a person] by the helping on of progress by utilizing experience."

26. Book III of Samuel Alexander's *Moral Order and Progress* (London: Trübner, 1889) is entitled "Dynamical—Moral Growth and Progress." Here is something of the flavor of Alexander's position: "progress is involved in the constitution of the ideal itself . . . the actual growth of the ideal" (263). So, "good is always ultimate . . . always in motion. There can therefore be no contrast of a 'good' and a 'best,' but only of a 'good' and a 'better.' Moral progress admits of only two degrees of comparison, the superlative being identical with the positive" (266). This adaptation is not of individual to environment or vice versa, but "can only be understood as a joint action of the individual and his environment, in which both sides are adjusted to each other" (271). The morality of a nineteenth-century Englishmen is no more highly developed than one in the twelfth century (292).

> The adjustment being once made, the good which results is absolutely good. Accordingly, there is no such thing as an absolute morality in comparison with which other conduct is variable and relative. The relativity of good conduct, instead of being a term of reproach, is in reality its highest praise: for it implies that the conduct takes account of those conditions, and no more than those conditions, to which it is meant to apply (293).

However, strictly speaking, we should not call Alexander and Dewey moral relativists. Rather, they reject moral absolutism and its counterpart, moral relativism, because these alternative outcomes of an inquiry are connected with what I have just referred to as an external, goal-oriented account of the meaning of progress. In *The Study of Ethics: A Syllabus*, Dewey outlaws what he calls the "relativity industry." According to him, even the relativist takes it for granted that "there is somehow a single, absolute standard of progress," but somehow "we aren't up to it yet" (*EW*, 4:317 n). I interpret Dewey to mean that the very formulation of a case for moral relativism takes for granted a theory of inquiry that assumes a successful, i.e., non-relativistic, theory must be based upon a "single, absolute standard."

27. *EW*, 4:261.

28. John Dewey, "The Theory and Institutions of Social Organization," Course 13 in Political Philosophy, from hand-written notes by Charles Horton Cooley, Michigan His-

torical Collections, Bentley Historical Library, University of Michigan, pp. 145–46 (editor's pagination). Cooley was then a student, and later a professor of sociology, at Michigan. For a later restatement of Dewey's account of progress, see *Human Nature and Conduct, MW*, 14:195, 197–98.

[Chapter 1.] General Considerations of the Nature of the Course: [The Antagonism Between Politics, Ethics, and Economics]

1. Political Philosophy is the theory of consciousness as social. It might be called Social Psychology for the use of other social sciences. The very concept of consciousness as social is so new that many difficulties are raised. That is why we have first to ask, is there a social consciousness?

2. We have now three distinct and more or less antagonistic spheres of social phenomena. 1. Politics. 2. Ethics. 3. Economics.[1] From the point of view of this separation, Ethics becomes one of two things, either an account at [of?] altruism or of metaphysical good and an attempt at man to reach [it].

3. In Economics, against altruism as motive, we have egoism. How to get the maximum gain with the least loss. This is connected on the ethical side with hedonism. On the other side we have a static, given individual as [over] against the metaphysical self of the ethical theory. The economic self has a very definite content, whereas the metaphysical self is empty of content as in Green. But at the same time it is just as much of an abstraction. The self is already made, given to you. It is not in process of construction or appreciation but already there. The reaction of the economic process into consciousness is ignored. The consciousness is taken as if the individual had been ready-made. The part which the economic reaction plays in bringing the self to consciousness is ignored. This is brought out in economic theory of value. It is represented as already given. On the side of wants, the wants are represented as already given. The wants are already given and all he wants is to satisfy those wants.

4. Another view is possible, that is, that the economic process makes the wants, brings to consciousness these wants. So in Ethics the parallel is a self, which is to be made; here it has been made. Further, Economics presupposes a fixed nature. The process of evolution of the commodities of nature, the utilization of nature, is ignored.[2] What Economics wants is to get all it can out of nature, instead of thinking that nature has been so much developed itself by these very processes. The economic idea is a relic of a time when consciousness was considered as injected miraculously. The world would have been what it is without consciousness and consciousness as consciousness would have been what it is and might have been formed in any other world. This is a purely external theory of consciousness.[3] It we take Politics as a third distinct social

[sphere], it is an attempt to get at concrete truth from a mixing of these two, that is, a man naturally egoistic has to adjust these processes so as to take some recognition of social rights. This is implicitly implied in the idea[4] of government. We make such an adjustment of egoistic tendencies that harm won't come to society; or, on the other side, that the government is [supposed] to foster the social tendencies of individuals.

5. The logic of these three positions is: Take first the position that Ethics deals with a metaphysical self; [second,] that Economics deals with a self already made; or [third,] that Politics is a means to harmonize. They are all pre-evolutionary and therefore pre-scientific. They were worked out in the eighteenth century, and preceded the historic evolutionary point of view. When the evolutionary point of view comes in, a reconstruction or supplement is necessary. Now we have no such thing as non-social man. The growth of science compels some reconstruction of the logic which splits up man and society. Besides, that reconstruction is going on in the sciences themselves because of the unsatisfactoriness of their present condition. Sociology, in its inception, was a response to this need of a more communistic theory (which had been split in these three departments) to break down this separation.

6. Two points were omitted under Ethics. When Ethics is thus discriminated, it is always built up on a theory of free will. The determinate content of the individual has been taken from him and placed in Economics and Politics, leaving only the form of a will. The other point is that Ethics, when thus defined, rests upon a psychological definition of the soul which sets it up as a fixed entity.

7. To come to the above where we left off: It was necessary that a pressure must arise within Ethics itself with new psychological ideas. The soul is no longer a fixed entity. The moment the self is considered as the progressive synthesis, the soul is no longer a fixed entity. All schools agree in saying there is a close connection between Psychology and Sociology. The true view of Sociology is not that it is a bridge on top, but that it is a genetic unity, that is, a unity out of which the different sciences were differentiated. The comprehensive social science must face the problem of how different facts get differentiated as well as how to correlate the different facts already differentiated.

8. This shows the need of fundamental categories and method adequate to this task of how the differentiation into Ethics, Politics, and Economics, from one another [was made]. First we must have genetic unity or origin; second, functional unity on the side to which it points. A new science is not cumulative,[5] but represents a new point of view, and has to reconstruct the categories at the basis of the other sciences. This shows the necessity of the historical rise of a new

point of view, and then the further necessity of a new intellectual point of view to correspond to the practical point. The idea of a social organism has been most used in the reconstructive work. Some authors used the idea of social organism simply as a bigger organism than the physical organism. This idea of social organism is again often used as if it were simply supplementary, distinct from the ethical, political, etc. Now society is either an organism or it is not. If it is, it affects all of these facts of ethics and economics; it is not something besides these.

9. Compare *American Journal of Sociology* for these two points of view: first article and last.[6] In the first [article] by Ross on "Social Control," sociological facts are viewed as accumulative. The assumption of Ross is that the individual is merely individual, and nonsocial. The problem is to see how man can be warped from his individual course. A psychological abstraction is involved in any such theory. He can't be the same individual after he has been considering the economics and politics of the world. New wants have been developed in the very process. Ross also makes the man's will something entirely distinct from feeling and judgment. The point of the criticism is that Sociology is built upon the psychology of the eighteenth century, which held that man had a soul as a special possession apart from other people. At that time, however, an organic society was not thought of. The notion of an organic society was the outgrowth of the same *Zeitgeist* out of which the new psychology came. If you write of the new society, you must also use the new psychology.

10. The same criticism may be made of Ward's article.[7] Feeling in regard to pleasure and pain is regarded as the sole cause for action. Biologically, this can't be proved. All action of animals and plants is hardly due alone to feeling of pleasure and pain. This is a presupposition concerning the individual.

11. Another point is the distinction which he makes between the object of nature, which is the building up of function or life; and of society, whose end is feeling. Feeling and function are distinct from each other. The object of the creature is feeling. Nature has no use for feeling, but by accident it comes in. The end of the individual is feeling of pleasure; but in doing this, he makes instruments and changes his environment, and these changes remain. So we have three things: the function, the object of nature; the happiness, the object of man; the effort, the object of evolution. All are distinct from each other. How can you make a different object of nature and of evolution, since nature has no meaning except in terms of evolution? In his own details he contradicts himself. [In] one place he says nature has no use for feeling, and again he says feeling is a means, [which] helps along the functioning of nature, and in this use it originated biologically. Now take the third statement that the object of evolution is

effort, that is, that nature and man, in getting pleasure, make efforts which lead to development. This simply shows that a thing has been objectified here which has been left out of the account above, that is, activity. Activity is presupposed both in nature and [in] the individual before you can get function or pleasure. All three put together make a good definition, but divided into three parts, [there] is an abstraction.

[Chapter 2. Turning Dualisms into Distinctions: Society/Nature, Subject/Predicate, Organism/Environment]

12. The above criticisms are a good way of showing us the fundamental problems of a science of sociology. Sociology is the science of the groups of social individuals. Now the question is, what is the relation of social philosophy to nature? This involves the question [as to] whether there is any relation at all. This will answer itself in the end.

13. Nature and society are supposed to be two different things without organic relation. The presupposition of this idea is that nature is regarded as merely subjective. This brings up the old question of subject and object. Must we take the point of view of separation,[8] or must we merge the social back into the objective, natural? Or is there a third way open by showing an organic relationship between them? The ideal of physical science or generalized cosmology is to explain everything in terms of redistribution of matter and motion, or mass and energy. There have been various attempts to reduce this duality of mass and energy into unity. For example, Descartes' attempt is to explain energy in terms of mass; and Leibniz' attempt to explain mass in terms of energy.

14. These attempts have not succeeded. The reason we can't explain one without another is because we have here constitution of thought, the subject and predicate. There is not simply an interdependence, but we view exactly the same set of facts from either point of view accordingly, that is, [according to] our interest and attention. One [the subject] represents the permanent and the other [the predicate] the variability.[9] That this is so and that the two shift according to interests indicates this distinction is teleological; that is, that the distinction falls within the sphere of means and ends. The definition of nature, as evolutionary, or the statement that nature's law is evolutionary, is simply realizing the interdependence of mass and energy. The principle there is what we always use in scientific investigation. When we state change in the old way we call it cause and effect; but when we come to recognize that the permanent and the variable are not different, but different phases of same,[10] it becomes the problem of differentiation, which is evolutionary. We no longer think of some things as static, and then [ask] the question how motion came in, as, for example, God starting the world. Fixed and variable are the same now, except viewed from different points. This is found in Spencer's "instability of the homogeneous."[11]

15. The process of differentiation in identity doesn't take place in any way, but has a definite law. It may be said that an organism is mass which is concen-

trated and replaced through the intensification and direction of energy. The whole process of evolution is an integration of matter everywhere. From this point of view a living organism represents a very peculiar concentration. What is meant by 'replaced' is plain. It is the idea of a circuit, of coming around again and repairing its own waste by what it does. This is what keeps it a living being. The main point that we get from studying the organism is the intensification of energy as necessary to the greater complexity of organism. The organism then can't represent anything but a stage in the process of nature. We have then broken down the fixed line between nature as dead and as organic.

16. The organism represents an accomplished adjustment if it is living at all. Organism as fixed is at the bottom of Spencer. Now the whole is evolving, not one alone. The process may be stated as the growing complexity and interrelation of the environment and organism. The bearing of the above upon social philosophy is upon the definition of the individual, as independent of the universe. Another question will develop further this: the relation of the will or ideals, and force. The dualism in the other sphere shows itself here, considering the will as purely spiritual and force as something outside of the will. The organism represents, from one point of view, a certain definition or focussing of the forces of nature, a certain attained equilibrium of the forces of the environment. The organism is a part of the environment, except from its own standpoint.

17. There is a relative distinction between organism and environment. We make this distinction. What is its scientific value? In the first place, the distinction must be made by a conscious being. The growth of a nonconscious animal is a simple redistribution of matter and motion; [there is an end] only as we set up an end to be attained. So the distinction between organism and environment can't be drawn from a physical standpoint, that is, where no end is assumed. The reason we set ends to plants and animals, is that we see they do objectively reach an end. The distinction we make for the plant, the conscious being makes for himself. The distinction, then, is teleological, that is, is made in regard to purposes. It is drawn after we have found a certain outcome has been reached, and in the looking back we say the things we see in the result have been working intentionally, and call that organism; the rest we call environment.

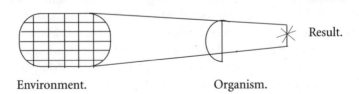

Environment.　　　　　　　Organism.　　　　Result.

Take an animal which is conscious. It wants to preserve itself. All things which tend immediately to do this end we call 'organism'. They don't exist off by themselves. These other elements which are formed to modify the immediate activities we call the 'environment'. The distinction is based again on this: Immediate activity is called organism; mediate activity is called environment.

18. Another point is necessary to complete the analysis. We do not make this distinction for another, nor yet for ourselves, except where there is some resistance in reaching the end. Let the process run smoothly, and we don't draw a line between the organism and environment, for example, walking. If it were not for the struggle for existence, we would not draw the distinction. Why don't we draw it for an acid or metal? Because we don't set up an end for it. Take the making of cloth. If we regard it as a result to which other things are uniformly related, we don't distinguish. But if we identify ourselves with the manufacture, we make the distinction. The manufacturer is the organism. But take the grower of cotton; here, he is the organism, and the manufacturer is part of the environment.

19. The three elements enter into [the] distinction.[12] 1. The organism is the changes toward an end. 2. Within this process certain factors tending toward this end immediately. 3. A certain relative conflict between the immediate and the mediate, that is, the necessity of an adjustment between these two in order to reach the end. For the term 'adaptation' of each to the other, let us substitute the term 'co-adaptation': of organism and environment to the function or end.

20. One point more[is needed] to make the transition to individuality: the point where the friction has been introduced, that is, where the immediate sees that it has got to make a struggle to reach the end. What happens? The mediate side withdraws. It identifies itself with the end, and looks on the environment as threatening. At the moment of friction, the organism sets itself up as an individual over against the environment. The relative opposition between organism and environment arises when the immediate and the indirect factors do not converge without a readjustment of both, that is, when the mediate side itself has to be readjusted in order to reach the end. The change, which is really a change of the whole, is explained always from the standpoint of one [side]. A mediation of the former environment and organism explains a change in the situation. The situation is the whole, viewed from the point of [view of] the environment; functioning is the whole from the point of [view of] the organism.

[Chapter 3. Individuality and the Cosmic Process: Consciousness as a Device for Turning Objects into Stimuli]

21. Situation and functioning represent the whole process. Organism as organism does not represent the whole; neither does environment as environment. In any case of re-adaptation or re-adjustment, the old environment as well as the old organism have to adapt themselves to the new environment. Compare this to a plant in a landslide. The functions which the plant has already worked out we call habits. These persist. They must persist, or the plant dies. On the other hand, these habits have got to change. Here is a basis for a conflict which may be called a conflict within function or within environment. It is a conflict between the constant and the variable, between habit and changed circumstances under which that habit must be exercised. This variable habit must come out of the old habit. This is a point too often overlooked, both on the social and the biological side. The old habit is responsible for the new situation.

22. That variation can not be described as anything but a mediation of the old habit. If we perceive mediation, we will avoid falling into many contradictions which seem to inhere in philosophical speculation. By 'mediation' is meant old activity continuing on, and assuming new aspects in old things.[13] Without this you have two schools of evolution, Spencer and [August] Weismann; [either] a spontaneous breaking loose or complete control by environment. The old function introduces new variations. The adaptation is from the old environment to the new environment; [it] adjusts the elements to each other. Stated on the side of function, the question of adaptation is a question of co-adaptation of organ and environment. It is a question of whether a function can take the consequences of its own activity, and utilize it. Give a being consciousness which has to meet this question, and let the necessity of new coordination arise, and the conscious being will identify itself with the formed habits. The organism will say: "I am the thing about which there is now question." The new factors or elements will be thrown outside the self. This is a distinction within the function, not outside of it. These which are at hand, which the individual already has, he calls himself; and these other things which he has not yet mastered, which he must yet deal with, is set off as not-self. The fallacy in current social writing is that these two are given as facts and the question [of adaptation] is all between the two. The distinction between the self and not-self is a distinction drawn within the consciousness of action, and relative to it. When it comes to a question of action, the individual has to abstract and fix the two; but the point

is, the division is only in reflection, and is within the action and for the action.

23. We can't stop with the statement that the self is identified with the accomplished part. In doing this act of abstraction, the self rarely becomes the end. The thing turns right over, and the self becomes the thing you have in view. In other words, you can't define conscious action without having the self regarded from two points of view. You must have the instrumental self, and the projected self. When the self is projected, then the environment becomes the means which [it] has got to get at, to realize itself. Then the objects become guides, etc. This relation is attention. While objects are stimuli to activity, they are not in consciousness. The conscious stimuli is something to be attained; they are what we are after, not what we have got. The corners of streets act as stimuli to turn without consciousness. If we lose our way they become conscious stimuli; that is, we are trying to turn the objects into stimuli, that is get our bearings. Objects become stimuli only in relation to an end-in-view.

24. What does consciousness mean in the development? It is the device for turning what opposes the self into stimuli for the advantage of the self. It is friction within a situation leading to disintegration of the coordination which led the organism to set itself up as an individual. In that tension the individual represents that phase of the old activity which was striving to persist and the organism the objects with which the individual cannot cope, and so is resistance; and in this way the self was projected as ideal. The problem, then, was how to turn these objections[14] into means for realizing the ideal self.

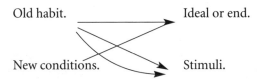

Old habit.   Ideal or end.

New conditions.   Stimuli.

From a biological point of view, we have the advantage of consciousness. Consciousness is that which enables conditions which otherwise would be hostile to functioning, to become stimuli, and thus become tributary to the functioning. Consciousness represents the ability to anticipate, and so the ability to interpret symbols, say of threatening circumstances. The change of conditions into stimuli is an activity by symbols.

25. *A digression: Space and time.* Space may be said to arise when the individual puts itself in the environment. If you think of a blackboard in its space relations, it is in relation to yourself. That is, you locate yourself in the space and make yourself a part of the environment. Space world is the outcome of looking at the agent as if it were part of the environment, and then asking what kind of an environment it is which has got yourself in it. Time arises when the en-

vironment is thrown in terms of the organism, that is, becomes a phase of your own activity. The reason that our experience takes the form of space and time relations is because we have to do both of these things.

26. We can't tell what means we have to use until we throw ourselves into the environment. Losing presence of mind is simply the inability to abstract from his own subjective state and look at himself as one of a number; as on a chess board. This impersonal attitude is essential to all practical activity. Why does one throw[15]environment in terms of organism? That is the side of defining the end, as the other was the means. According to the different ends-in-view we will apperceive it in very different ways. If we define the means only in terms of [an] end, then space and time are correlative. You can't define space except in terms of time, and vice versa. What happens when you locate the University in reference to the house where you live? You, in this room, you put [yourself] on one side; and the house on the other. In the time view, one postulates objects as distinct, in space, and then thinks of them as converging to a unity.

27. To return to the nature of individuality in relation to the whole cosmic process, we see that it has two aspects. On one hand, there is the individual considered as adjusted; a certain equilibrium of forces, an attained adjustment. The universe, in other words, focuses. The individual is so much concentrated universe. This corresponds to the freely acting habit and unconsciously, so far as his environment as against himself was concerned, this might be called the objective individual. He is marked off from his environment. This is a rhythmic process in all development. It represents the constant factor as against the variable. We might also call it the functional individual; or better, the structural individual.[16]

28. If we take the phase of reconstruction, we get the tensional individual, instead of the functional (structural) individual. This is the variable, while the other is the permanent. It is the transitional species. That is the reason we find the transitional species gone in natural evolution. They are [part] of reconstruction, and therefore represent a process, and should not be found [as] objective product.[17] The search for absolute continuity is a contradiction. Wherever you get nature to look at, it is some special fact, and not the process. The process is continuous, but the products must be discrete. This does not mean that there are two individuals, but when we reflect on the process of individuality, it breaks up into these two phases.

29. [1.] Taking up first, in consciousness as such, objects which possess two types of value. One of these is a saturation value, and the relation of the individual to that value is that of absorption. Speaking from structural form, objects possess this saturated value, which is the summation of the previous development of consciousness. In a popular way we call it the intellectual atmosphere,

or *Zeitgeist*. Every individual is born into a world which already has an intellectual atmosphere. There are certain characteristics which are more or less common to all human beings since they are an inheritance from the prehuman age. If we accept an evolutionary theory, we have noticed that once they did not have the same value. Once they had an indicative value, instead of a saturation value.

30. [2.] The second is the index or pointing function called indicative value. That is, they were signs of certain kinds of reaction[s] which the animal should make. Even with us, taste and odor act as stimuli to action as well as qualities in the substances. Then in the animal it is conceivable that it might be only that, and so they have merely the indicative value. On the basis of evolution you can't account for origin and selection of intellectual and aesthetic qualities except on the theory that once they were not simply intellectual or simply aesthetic, but had the indicative character of stimuli to action.

31. The saturation value corresponds to the adapted individual, to his environment. There is no tension. All the individual has to do is to absorb it. So far as the individual has to reconstruct the environment and make[18] a new situation out of the old, he abstracts himself from it, takes objects as indexes; and saturation value is the immediate value, and indicative value is the mediate value. The saturation values fix the plane of the social consciousness at any given time. The quantity and quality of such values determine the psychical environment of the individual; that is, they determine the plane on which the individual acts. One phase of saturation has been pointed out as the inherited psychical product of the ages before: his sensory qualities, as eye, ear, etc.

32. Further [on in organic development] is language. The individual is receiving a certain view of these values through the medium of language. This is the starting point of the individual consciousness. The study of that constitutes ethical statics;[19] that is, that plane is the statics in reference to which the change in the individual takes place. Statics does not here designate something fixed. Statics as a category means rather the attained organization taken as a basis for further functioning. If we take the point of imitation made so much of by Baldwin,[20] that is a phase of the absorption or assimilative attitude of the individual. Just because we assume these saturation values which the individual has breathed unconsciously from the dawn of life, it is difficult to get an idea of its [their?] importance. The relation of any one individual to this saturation plane, is almost like that of one particular plant to the whole physical surroundings. So the tendency is to throw it into the variable side. Because the individual consciousness is so largely a given or presumed thing, it fixes the level of social consciousness as a reality, and not as mere metaphor. (See also Grote's Hist. Greece, Syll. of Ethics.)[21]

[Chapter 4. Putting Content into Social Consciousness: Objects as Indicative (Organism) or Appropriative (Tools)]

33. If there is a social consciousness, it must be found in the individual and not somewhere outside, as in some present day argument on social consciousness. The question comes now: What are we to do with the indicative value of the reconstructing individual? That definitely marked phase of individual consciousness where we get self-consciousness as against object-consciousness, marks the nodal point in social evolution. He represents the progressive variation of the social consciousness. This initiating movement which the individual takes represents a new factor in the social consciousness.

34. To analyze further the social consciousness: It has been propounded that there is a psychical or subjective environment which influences the individual. This is a step in the right direction, but it is liable to be wrongly used; that is, that it is something over and above the physical environment. The entire environment of a conscious being is psychical. Any physical environment is psychical for a conscious being. The kind of nature we live in is a strong determining factor of our psychical life.

35. The value that the physical environment has in the psychical will obviously be socially determined. If we could draw a fixed line between the physical and the psychical, then we might talk of a person being individualistically determined. But it is not so. In other words, plants must assume a different attitude to a society with high agricultural development than in a pre-agricultural society.

36. No fixed lines can be drawn. The value of different objects to the individual depends upon the social life of the time. Take as illustration the evolution of myths. Why do all races of people begin with animal and plant myths, and then include meteorology myths, and then more and more of natural phenomena? It will be found that it is paralleled by the economic and social condition of the people. When people live on animals and plants, their minds are full of those things. We say that our consciousness has developed from that time, but don't think that the world has changed. But that is not true. The world is different.

37. The easiest way to put content to the social consciousness—what this course aims to do—is to show that the whole world is saturated with values which society has given it. The value which fills the consciousness at the time, the saturation value, determines the social plane. And any change that takes

place must take place in reference to this plane. It is analogous to Weber's law in psychology, and to marginal utility in economics.[22]

38. Whether we take the appropriative activity, or [the] indicative value, certain phases of the objects present themselves as stimulating or calling out action, and others present themselves as restricting the activities which have been called out. So far as the object has the stimulating phase, we may call it an organ of action; so far as it has the other we may call it a tool.

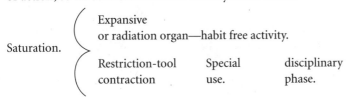

Saturation.
Expansive or radiation organ—habit free activity.

Restriction-tool contraction | Special use. | disciplinary phase.

39. *[Social Statics]* Both [expansion and constriction are] combined again to constitute social statics. An object is an organ so far as we can function through it freely at the time. As a tool, we mean that we can use it to [achieve] some end. By saying that the above constitutes the social order in [the] psychical environment, it is meant that [it is] what does give the coherence or structural form to special types in so far as they have those values.

40. The habit organ represents the rights side, and the other the duty. But these have no meaning except in relation to values of objects. Take the matter of property right;[23] it is the assumption of the values of objects; objects assuming, on one hand the mere stimulating value, and on the other hand the controlling value. The necessity of definite property rights is that these relationships may take definite shape. If we take the indicative side, and assume that objects have the same two types of value, [1] on the side of stimulation what the objects set up is variation by initiation, and not new habits. The object simply calls forth some new activity. Psychologically, it is the impulse as opposed to habit. [2] On the restrictive side, we have invention or adaptation, with reflection as the psychology phase. The object presents a new problem.

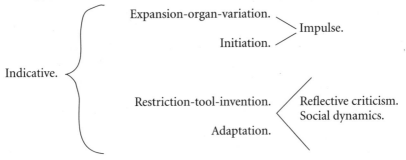

Indicative.
Expansion-organ-variation. Initiation. — Impulse.
Restriction-tool-invention. Adaptation. — Reflective criticism. Social dynamics.

41. *[Social Dynamics]* This [diagram] will give us, combined, the [two factors in] social dynamics. The conflict in Greek life is reflected in Socrates and Plato. The latter's ideas were highly conservative, to keep things where they were, and yet the means to be used were reflection and criticism. This is a direct contradiction, so [there] was breakdown.

42. Referring to [the] two phases, the adapting and adapted individual, it should be stated that the terms 'stimulus' and 'control' are used in different sense[s]. We who look back on the process as adapted, look at them as objects. But not so at the time of adapting. Only after we get out of an activity do we become conscious of what was stimulus and what was control. At the time, the individual is not conscious of what the control is. If he were, it would show questionings, that is, it would not then be control.

43. As long as a stage is absolutely dogmatic, it isn't dogmatic from its own standpoint. It only is to the looker-on, or critic. As long as the structural phase predominates, then there will be no distinction between the subjective and objective. But as soon as the individual begins to question, the distinction begins to emerge. The psychology of the process is that of finding the facts which stimulate him to activity and the principles by which he governs it.

[Chapter 5. The Individual as Instrument of Social Development: No Essential Opposition Between the Individual and Society]

44. The bearing of this upon political activity is this: the same thing which makes the conscious distinction between subjective and objective is also the process by which the conscious distinction of the individual to society is made. The individual who has set himself off from society is making himself subjective.

45. There will be three periods, all development. 1. Practically conscious (of the value of the activity only). The activity enlarges and resistance arises within it. 2. The individual has to define himself. The Socratic period: know thyself— to know [a.] the stimuli to action and [b.] the standard which had limited action. This arises from the emergence of the necessity of analyzing the previous falling into [these] two parts. 3. The attained activity is unified, which is just like the first stage, only it is now consciously a unity. It has the value in itself of the contrast of the previous stage. An illustration: Every Russian peasant is not conscious that he is living under despotism. They [the Russian peasants] have never questioned the relation of themselves to the state. Let these [peasants] question what they might do, and the person begins to criticize the state of affairs of himself. Let the unity be attained again, that is, get a democratic community, and he will again be but the expression of his state. The average mortal uses history simply to get a background for his present state, and thus get more value in it. The relative opposition in consciousness between the individual and his associated activity arises when the individual finds it necessary to bring to consciousness his activity, that is, the stimuli to control and the standard of control. The fallacy comes in when this apparent opposition is taken for an absolute opposition, and an historical value for an inherent value.

46. Locke, Hume, and Hobbes were individualistic because they were becoming conscious of themselves as individuals, as distinct initiators.[24] The feudal system was just broken up, and they interpreted that. Not a class,[25] but the individual was an independent actor. This does not mean mere disintegration. The individual has become a unity. This opposition between individual and society is simply an illustration of historical perspective. When either the individual or society is passing rapidly through changes, the negative aspect comes first to consciousness, and the harmony only later.

47. What we have seen so far is that the individual may be considered as a concentrated situation. Also that the adapted individual marks one limit in the rhythmic process. The other is that where the situation comes reflectively to consciousness as a means to its further development. When objects are no longer self-sufficing things but clues to [a] further line of activity, [consciousness] takes [a] negative attitude to the old association. The fallacy of setting the individual absolutely over against society is the neglect of the fact that the individual, by taking a negative attitude towards past habits, is only the instrument for social advancement. This makes [for] a most close relation between individual and society. That is, social progress is always precarious except so far as it becomes a method in the individual's consciousness, abstracted from the content.

48. If we ask why the history of civilization begins with the Greeks, we get the answer here. The Greeks brought to consciousness the [idea of social] progress. The life of the Orient had not been consciousness but the result of the progress. We have accordingly two phases of ethics, one of which is social ethics. As such it would discuss values attained in any social organization. It would treat individuals simply as carriers of these social habits. He is saturated or absorbed in social life. On the other hand, psychological ethics would throw emphasis on the individual in whom these social habits were focused. [It] would ask what the method of the social life was as it functions through the individual.

49. We will make the distinction one way or another according to the place of our interest. On the saturation side, habit; use of habit. Social ethics is the theory of habits, and use of habit. On the educational side, reflection, impulse. Psychological ethics deals with the above. The relation of individuals and society can't possibly have two things: individuals and society. After you have opposed every individual to society, where is your society to oppose them? What we do have, is the opposition of different phases to each other, an individual as a member of a class finds himself opposed by individuals of certain other classes. One individual is never opposed to another—so far as they are members of society as a whole. But so far as society is disintegrated into classes, individually[26] one class opposes another. The function of this opposition of individuals within the classes is to do away with opposition between classes. This is a further statement of the fact that the individual, so far as he takes negative attitudes to his past life, is an instrument to further development. Opposition is a stimulus, and to define the stimulus adequately it must be done in terms of the whole. It has been said before that the value of consciousness was the power it gave to the individual to turn its barriers into stimuli—new in so far as the social opposition becomes a bearer of facts to consciousness.

[Chapter 6. Competition Replaces Conflict in the Development of Wider Associations]

50. The significance of the nervous system is that it enables the various parts to coordinate on the basis of an end, while the organism so far as it has no nervous system can unify itself only on the basis of superial physical force. Give an animal a nervous system and it means that these critical stimuli are reduced to being claims and the nervous system is the umpire which decides which claim is superior. The nervous system is a scheme for translating things in terms of past into things in terms of future. In the nervous system on the peripheral side, we have continued development of the sense organ. On the central side, is one of integration. The third phase is growth of connecting fibers. The lack of a nervous system means that the preponderance of discharge depends on a superior amount of stimulus. The opposite, then, never has the social value as such, but it is through the stimulus it gives to consciousness that it has a value.

51. For example, what has been the value of war? Sometimes it is deified as an instrument of advancement. Contrary [to that], it is said war is simply a hindrance to development. So far, war remains purely physical; it is a hindrance. But in so far as the friction induces to reflection [which is] translated over into thought, in so far, it may become an instrument of social progress. That is, war [as] anticipated leads to precaution. This is purely on the intellectual side and not an overt act. Even though this is a function of opposition, does it really do that? [The] answer is: How far has society a nervous system? First question: Is society organic? Second question: Is society organized? This last is: How far has it got some instrumentality by which it anticipates possible frictions so far that it can coordinate them on the basis of an end?

52. In the stage of adaptation of individual to his surroundings, we have seen that the individual participates in society and also contributes to society.[27] Now every such adaptation is at the expense of segregation. It marks an objective isolation and segregation of such a social group; that is, the social group can't adapt itself to the whole environment, but selects a local environment and adapts itself to that, neglecting the rest. It forms for itself the habits which are able to cope with a more or less marked off and particular environment. For example, a social group on the seashore grows up as a seafaring people. The earlier forms of social adaptation, because they must be made on the basis of comparatively local environment, will represent one-sided values from the standpoint of the whole. On the basis of such an adaptation, one of these groups will develop

powers which will carry it beyond its local restrictions. The seafaring people will make boats and go beyond the shore to fish. That is, the habits they have developed to complete use of their situation lead them beyond that situation. Both habits on the subjective side, and instruments on the subjective[28] side, develop to make a social group master of their environment, actually, must lead them beyond [it].

53. The individual reflects the social status of his time—without individual rights in primitive times. Social conflicts don't arise within the group for the individual is more or less parasitic [upon the group]. Through the use of habits built up to extend the environment, [the friction] may easily lead to conflict. We have then the segregation of different social groups on the basis of different local environment, then complete mastery of environment, then conflict between these various segregated groups on the basis of trying to enlarge the environment. The movement underlying the conflict has positive value. It is the symptom of enlarged environment and again of contact between different groups.

54. So long as groups are, physically, entirely separated there can be no physical disintegration. Through this contact of previously segregated groups, the competitive phase of social action arises. If the conflict is purely physical, it cannot be of value as a stimulus. When the groups attempt to define to themselves the end [to] which they wish to react, the conflict becomes a competition. The unconscious life of habits, in other words, is replaced by a life of reflection. The group no longer unconsciously goes on living, but is conscious of the end and analyzes the present situation in the light of that end.

55. That competitive phase represents the relatively conscious adaptation of the social group for the work for which it is most fitted. On the side of the organism it represents the securing of an advantageous variation, the starting out on . . .[29] . . . of the environment, it represents a better utilization of its forces, that is, the competitive as resistance is the stimulus to initiative and to reflection. The main point about this competitive phase of social life is to see its function, to see what it is for. Considering it as an evil is due to a misapprehension of these. Competition always exists for the escape from competition, and the significance of the struggle for existence is to put one above that continual competition.

56. In so far as the process is an evolutionary process, it is a continual process of getting above a previous competitive plane. The competition becoming too prominent a feature of the situation means not evolution, but impeding of the process; it represents congestion. The movement of growing individualization on one side and greater utilization of environment on the other, is what we have. The competition has this fierce aspect at the critical point always, just before the favorable variation has occurred. Those who regard competition as essentially

evil and cooperation an absolute ideal, [please] do answer this question: What is the occasion of a new variation? What is the stimulus to progress in a regime that has done away with competition?

57. Conflict, it has been said, arose from segregation or isolation. That segregation arises because a local environment is select, and the adaptation goes on in relation to it. The ends are thus limited. The habits in agreement with these limited ends are more or less fixed. The social consciousness of such a [limited] group, as a whole, though it is coherent, is limited and rigid. The coherency and consistency has been gained at the expense of narrowness on the quantitative side and undue rigidity on the qualitative side. The conflict arises because of the social situation becoming more unified (two groups are becoming one) and habit is growing wider. The rigidity is because we identify ourselves with the part as fixed. If we are looking at the whole situation, what looks like disintegration is greater unifying. Disintegration is always the negative side of the formation of more comprehensive unity. We are so accustomed to stand[ing] on the part that we failed to see the whole of which it is a part. Conflict is mere conflict, when we ignore the process as it is developing and identify ourselves with one of the organisms that is being developed in the process.

58. This conflict between local social groups always reacts on the groups. A division is taking place within each of the old groups at the same time these groups are breaking down barriers between themselves. The great industrial individualization that has been going on (competition of different groups) made a world market; and the old habit of producing for just so many (the one segregated group) was shaken up, and the industry becomes carried on on the basis of reflection, invention and to build up a market. This threw the individual into relief, just as the individual always appears at the turning point of habit. What we have is on the one hand the formation of a larger group, and on the other a recoil from the contact, shaking the old individuals from their niches, and giving rise to variation. Any segregated group must be a nonprogressive group so far as it is adapted to its local environment. Progress comes in when, because of a larger situation, the old individuals have to break from their old and make a place for them[selves] in the new.

59. Before, the stimulus was present, but as a stimulus it was not conscious. Now we have to get stimuli out of them and direct activity on basis of that. Necessary movement is towards humanity on one side and the individual on the other. You can't have your individual completely differentiated until you have the widest possible association; that is, the individual can't have all his powers stimulated unless he acts as a member of the largest possible association. If the end is narrow, it will restrict the number of powers called into activity. It is ob-

vious that there will be critical periods in development when segregated groups will have been done away with and the new will not yet have its constitution. At such critical stages, the unity is not seen and the appearance is that of confusion and conflict. The old definiteness and coherence is gone and the clearness of vision is not sufficient to see the new unity that has formed itself. The conflict between individuals is simply the correlate of the lack of definiteness, the constitution of the larger group. They come into conflict because they don't see their relation to each other in this larger associated life.

[Chapter 7. Is Society an Organism?]

60. If we define 'organism' from the idea of calling anything an organism, society must be conceived as organic. We must use this category in order to understand the facts. The reason for this will be seen in studying the two main facts in organism. One is the thought of a unity or whole which gives meaning to the activity of all its points, and the other is that these parts are economical centers for maintaining, through continual reconstruction, the activity of the whole.

61. It is useless to discuss whether society is an organism or not until we have defined what [an] organism is, that is, on what ground we call anything an organism. What is involved in the concept of an organism is underlined in the two-fold fact above. The latter half of the above definition has two phases. A certain amount of diversity is included in the idea of an organism. There is the phase of: 1. Specialization; 2. Interdependence.

62. Three phases of activity are always going on in any organic life. 1. The activity which takes in, or nutritive activity. 2. The elaborative, or digesting. 3. The depurating process of excluding useless matter, and assimilating the useful. Specialization and interdependence are correlative, and cannot be separated. That is, the energy necessary to expel waste product has to be made good by the nutritive and elaborate processes. The first element in the definition makes the difference between organism and machine. The machine shows the specialization of interdependent parts, but the whole does not react in its constituent elements. Even in plants it is much less marked than in man. This is why society is a higher organism than the individual. It has a more definite value. It is involved in all this in that the unity is one of action and not one of existence or form. The latter is found in the inorganic as well as in organic. It is functional unity. Moreover, any particular thing is conceived of as a unity only when for the time being it is looked on as organic.

63. The various objections to the theory of society as an organism may all be reduced to two general heads. First, the point by Spencer (*Principles of Sociology*[30]) that in biological organism the parts are all subservient to another part. The nervous system alone has final value, that is, has feeling. While society as a whole has no consciousness and the units have the feeling. That is, society has no social consciousness. (Vol. I, Part II, pp. 448–80.) Second, from the opposite school which objects that the concept of organism is only biological and ultimately physical, while society is ethical and spiritual. That is, the concept of

organism goes back like all natural concepts to the idea of force. The unity of society, involving will and personality, transcends the idea of force. (See also writings of F. M. Taylor of Michigan University, M. T. Harris. Both have the idea of society as spiritual.[31])

64. There are two problems: 1.Is society thoroughly organic, that is, has it sensori? 2. What is the relation of the biological phase of the organism to the ideal or spiritual? That is, what is the antithesis between force and will? Is will something that supervenes upon the organism, or is it the completest expression of the principle of organism? Has society a consciousness? Spencer attributes consciousness to the nervous system because it is the necessity [needed] to [have] sensations in any part of the body. But the real question is: How does the nervous system act in reference to species (parts)? But it is as foolish to say that consciousness is there as to say that the explosion lays [i.e., causes] the match because the powder does not explode until the match is applied. The nervous system is not different from other tissue, only differently differentiated.

[Chapter 8.] Relation of Individual Organ to Organism as Whole

65. Consciousness is always referred to an individual organ. The eye sees, the finger feels, etc. This is because consciousness is not located anywhere. The lower the consciousness, the more it is referred to the organism as a whole instead of any special organ. Really it is not the eye that sees, but the organism through it; that is, the organ is the organism specified or differentiated. What does this reference of value to some specific organ indicate? It means a balance between the specialization and interdependence. Or it means a balance between the stimulating and inhibitive forces of nature. In absolutely undifferentiated organism, there could be no consciousness. The consciousness has more content to the degree in which there is the specialization of an organ on one side, and on the other that specialized organ stimulates other organs and is controlled by their controlled stimulation of it.

66. We brought out that consciousness is always referred to a particular organ. The content of consciousness thus referred expresses the organism as a whole. The "what" of consciousness is always the expression of the organism as a whole. The "that" of it is individual. The balance between individual organ and organism as a whole must be maintained.

67. Take as an illustration the perceptual development of consciousness of color. At outset the color consciousness is not defined in any sense. A child is not conscious of any reference of it to his eye. The color is rather a thrill of the whole organism. So long as it is thus diffused, it lacks richness of content or meaning. In the next stage the child takes the red color as the adjective of a ball which he is in the habit of playing with. New experience is marked off. In being thus defined, it has more, not less, of the value of other experiences in it.

68. In the next plane of development, the scientific man, red denotes a certain metal, sun as found by spectrum analysis: now the extent is very small. Being thus defined, it is saturated with all the rest of scientific knowledge which man has. This illustrates the principle that the growth in definiteness means growth in specialization. And growth in richness of content which is correlative with the above shows the extent to which the whole organism is expressing itself in the individual organ. The difference between mere seeing as stimulus to subsequent activity and scientific or aesthetic seeing is that in the last the seeing stimulates other organs which return on the seeing, stimulating it to con-

trol and modify it. So any seeing in human consciousness necessitates such a co-ordination.

69. When there is seeing, and that stimulates other activities which react on the seeing again but does not control it, we get hallucination. The normal consciousness represents the balance between two extreme types: animal, where it is just serial with no interaction; and hallucination, where there is interaction, but no control. This also explains immoral action. All error is the same type, that is, failure to balance between immediate and mediate activities. The different organ stimulations are to re-stimulate the immediate organ without also controlling it. Psychical deafness and blindness are good illustrations of this principle. Man may see colors and forms but they are nothing to him, because the connection with other centers are atrophied and the reinforcements are gone.

70. Taking now individual and society as correlative with organ [and organism] in a biological organism: The ordinary theory is that the individual has his consciousness given to him. But this is not the case. His consciousness depends on how he can stimulate others and how again they react on him. Individual activity does not give consciousness by itself. Consciousness is interpretation of that activity by and through its social interaction or relationships. The individual is not conscious simply because he acts, but because he recognizes the place of the activity in the whole. While the consciousness is always the interpretation of impulse through its mediation, if we take the content of the mediation it is always social.

71. The growth of consciousness is due to the way A acts on B, C, etc., and how they react again on A. Learning to walk is of the same sort. In animal types of consciousness there is simply the serial type, but A would never absorb and make part of itself the return stimulations from B and C. The whole question of social organization is a question of organizing stimuli and responses.

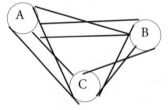

It is a question on the individual side, A, the stimulation of the individual. On the social side, [the question is] how far are channels of stimuli organized so they react on special stimuli in a way to control it as well as re-stimulate it, that is, give the individual activity a definite place in the whole? All mechanisms of society [are] not so many various things, but modes in which the one question is being worked out; that is, all processes and activities of society fundamentally are to be regarded on the basis of the part they play in constituting this social sensorium. The social sensorium is an organization of stimuli and responses of various individuals in the social group.

72. Going back to saturated and indicative phase of activity: When the process balances easy, that is, when outgoing activity has not become so definite that it does not take effort to modify it, we have saturated point. When it has taken such definite shape that its modification means reconstruction, and the individual is thrown out of the overt act, we have indicative. The social process is one that makes as much for individualization as for association. The associated phase represents the static phase, not in a sense of fixed, but, status of things. The reflection and experimentation bringing in new values gives us the dynamic phase. The whole problem of social life is the organization of the social consciousness on the basis of stimuli and inhibition.

[Chapter 9.] Three Social Sciences:
[Economics, Politics, Ethics]

73. The ethical question is the question of the extent and manner in which the various activities are translated over into conscious values. It is a question not of a particular mechanism in which this control goes on, or structure in which a mechanism is centered, but of how far and in what way the activities come to consciousness and in what way they are present as conscious values.

74. We may say ethics deals with the ends or ideals involved in these reciprocal activities, provided we do not mean ideals objectively[32] aimed at, but the ideals as they are reflected into consciousness. There are no moral values except in consciousness, so to take any value as value is to raise the ethical question.

75. 1. The economic phase is a question of mechanism or machinery by which individuals reciprocally stimulate and control each other. When we ask how an individual stimulates and controls, we have a question of economics. 2. If we ask concerning the structure of the organism through which this reciprocal relation and response is exercised, and through which the conscious values are mediated, we have the political question. 3. [The] ethical question is a question of ends. Economics is question of means. Politics is a question of adjustment of the two, or the technique. Ethics gives the idea of freedom, that is, the amount of value of social activities which is absorbed.

76. On the side of Economics it is demands. On the side of Politics it is the assumed rights[33] of individual and organ; it is goods, powers, claims. On the side of readjustment, Ethics gives us responsibility, Economics gives us supply, and Politics obligations. The organization of social consciousness is to maintain the equilibrium between freedom and responsibility, demand and supply, rights and obligations. Responsibility can be only in the exercise of freedom, that is, you can't go on except on past habit, so one can exercise demand only. Virtue, of the supply he already has. Effective demand is simply supply functioning. Rights which one can exercise defend a position he has in the organism. It is the relationship involved in that position, and they are the obligations one has to meet. Every right means an obligation. It means an activity and therefore means something for a person to do. We call it a right when we see that it is referred to the individual's own consciousness. It is a duty or obligation when we take content of obligation and ask what is involved in it.

77. To go again to the ethical side. There follows the impossibility of any abstract ideal or standard. The attempt to discover a law which is the law is fu-

tile. The ethical question is: What are the values recognized as we go on? It is a functional value, and we are victims to ethical fallacy when we abstract and set it up by itself. There is no ethics outside the ethical process.

78. We have two aspects of ethics: one the historical, which is an account of various types of values, progressively realized; and psychological ethics, or the statement of the form of process by which reconstruction of values occurs. The search for abstract value outside of process lands us into something which is neither psychological nor historical ethics, but metaphysical ethics in the sense that it transcends the process. The question of ends and force in volition is only relative or functional distinction. The measure of force or idea of force is intelligible only in reference to some end. Economics does its selecting on side of force, and ethics does its selecting on side of end.

79. Politics deals with anatomy of structure. The structural side is necessarily assumed in all economics, but it must not be disregarded. The people who manage economics are the political institution. The same fact may be ethical, economical, or political, according to the point of view.

[Chapter 10.] Structure of Social Organization

80.[1.] An institution is a social habit. Sovereignty is the habit of these habits, not as another habit but the life habit from which all special habits are differentiated. A habit is an end executing itself. It is neither mere mechanism nor mere idea, but is the idea or end mechanized. Or it is organic machinery which subserves a function. From these follows: It is impossible to set sovereignty over against special institutions. It is the organized effective unity of the institutions. In other words it is but another name for the social organism taken on the side of organs through which it realizes itself.

81. 2. It is impossible to identify sovereignty with force.[34] It is a forceful idea.

82. 3. Institutions or habits have two aspects, one as specialized differentiation of sovereignty or social habit marking what we would get if we took a cross-section of social consciousness. This is the positive or legal aspect of institutions. It is the extent to which each of these institutions expresses sovereignty. The other phase is found in the fact that each special institution is only one differentiation and not isolated habit, and so has to adjust itself to other habits. If we take the defined side, then we have the positive phase. Take the flexible side and we have the moral phase.

83. For sake of convenience we may distinguish between category of organ and category of member in every organism. When the eye gives expression to the organism it represents an organ. When it is considered as subject to [the] whole it is a member. Now institution taken as organ is the positive side. Taken as member it represents the flexible side.

84. 4. Every institution is habit and therefore sovereignty as a whole is defined in law, that is, law is the functional direction of the habit. This law is determined on one side in right, that is, stimuli involved in the exercise of habit; and on the other side in obligations, which are the inhibitions and control in the operation of habit. We will use law in the sense of Roman justice, that is, not as "all obligation" but as both rights and obligation.

85. It is quite common to define sovereignty as having its power in the exercise of supreme force—instead of force of an organized power, which means force determined by an end. Therefore sovereignty is set up against other powers. See also Salter, *Anarchy or Government*.[35] "State sovereignty is coercive power. Voluntary powers are persuasive." This shows the antithesis plainly. He holds that in the ideal state, sovereignty would be done away [with]. Then people would do the best they could. Now, is it possible to make any such distinc-

tion between a voluntary act of will and force? Can we eliminate the content of enforcing, itself, from a decision of the will? If we can, what becomes of our will?

86. The fallacy of explaining sovereignty as force *per se* arises there. All will is forceful. Will means the struggle to realize one's own ideals. As society developed, it was found advisable to regulate this force, that is, just as end is defined, the force must be defined. This process of the regulation of force, which is intrinsic part of every voluntary association, comes to be abstracted. One organ is differentiated to do the controlling work for the sake of economy, for example, [as with] an umpire in a game.

87. Now the fallacy arises when we consider all forces inherently belonging to this one organ. The aim of Salter's book is to prove that strong government is necessary now, so that they will reach the point when no government is needed. When you make any such arbitrary distinction, you either have an organism with[out] organs or on the other side, organs without being organs of any organism. It is the historical fallacy again. That is, take the outcome of process as fixed and then set it up to explain the very process of which it is the outcome.[36] See also *Quarterly Journal of Political Science*, Vol. '93, or '94 article on "Austin's Theory of Sovereignty." For historical statement of sovereignty, see also Green, "Political Rights"; Maine, Chapter 12, "Early Historical Institutions."[37]

88. There are two general antitheses running through the idea of sovereignty from Hobbes to the present. One of these is the difference between unlimited and limited force; and the other, the location or residence of sovereignty. In Hobbes, Spinoza, Rousseau, Cornewall Lewis, you find it stated that force which constitutes sovereignty is unlimited. In Locke, Austin (Section on Jurisprudence) you find that the amount of force is limited. As to residence of force, Hobbes, Locke, and Austin hold that location of sovereignty is in a numerically limited portion of society. Rousseau holds that sovereignty is in society as a whole.[38]

[Chapter 11.] Political Sovereignty: Legal, Moral, Popular, National[39]

89. Every attempt to mark off legal sovereignty has failed because it is simply a device for analysis. The sense in which legal sovereignty may be said to be supreme force is that as supremacy of organized force it is unlimited. A good many writers write against unlimited power of sovereignty because when it has ceased to do the right thing, there ought to be the right of revolution.

90. If we take the side of the problem as to the resistance of sovereignty and take Rousseau, who holds that sovereignty is general will, and Austin, who holds that it is located in a certain number of persons: In Rousseau's view, government becomes simply a servant of sovereignty. The question is here, how shall sovereignty operate? Rousseau says that every individual has a social and a particularistic side. In the first capacity he helps to make up the general will; in the other, he is the servant of general will.

91. All law must represent the assent of every single individual in society. The practical difficulty is here very plain. The way he gets over this is that when people vote they vote whether the law agrees with the general [will], not whether it must be a law. Then if the majority vote "yea", it shows that the others were mistaken. This of course is simply an evasion.

92. Now take Locke. He holds that government is situated in a certain number, but is to be used for public good, and when it ceases to carry out the function for which it was created . . .[40] But this puts the real sovereignty in the people.

93. We have three difficulties: identifying sovereignty with supreme force, identifying it with general will, and identifying it with a limited portion of society. Hobbes says it is supreme force and located in a few. Locke says that it is located in a few, but must be in the interest of the whole. Rousseau says that it is for all and resides in all. Cf. May '94, *Political Science Quarterly*.[41]

94. Austin's statement is that a definite number of individuals must be sovereign because an indefinite number could not give laws. This is in extreme antithesis to Rousseau, who denied even a representative government. Austin's statement is also insufficient. The question at once arises how it is that a determinate portion gets the power away from the rest? Or, again, why one determinate body yields such obedience? In splitting society thus, there is no answer to the above question. It is a mere matter of accident. His weak point is this very thing, and gives no basis for discriminating why one is as it is and the other [is

as it is]. Such a theory is destructive of the whole idea of social organization. Austin implicitly recognizes that and says that the reason one set [i.e., determinate body] obeys is because of the utility. Excepting as we do refer to some larger reality as [including?] society as governing and as society as governed, we get into anarchy. There would be continual striving for the powers. It really does not give a society at all, but two.

95. Austin is further obliged to hold that constitutional law is not law at all, but advisory precepts. The constitutional law is the law which determines the government. But if government is sovereign you have either got to say that there is another sovereign over this sovereign, or else that the sovereign chooses to observe them but has no legal obligation.

96. The same difficulty holds when we study the development of the constitution. Every change, according to Austin, must be revolutionary. The institution of sovereignty has to be instituted from something other than government itself. Any change is of the same nature. If we take the other phases of law (municipal) what is the relation of law in this sense to sovereignty if it resides in a definite portion of society? According to Austin this whole phase is an expressed command from this definite portion, or sovereign. It would be more rational to say that the government was to see that these ordinary rights were carried out, not that [it] made them. Every right of a child is due to the sovereign according to Austin. This is the *reductio ad absurdum* of Austin's theory.

97. History shows us that law is simply the crystallization of custom; we get back to the logical fact of [the] outset [of law]. That theory of the sovereign as determinate portion of society makes an irretrievable dualism in society itself, and so destroys the value of law and conformity to law. Contrary [to that], Rousseau's theory of purely general will won't work because it has no organs of exercise.

98. Now do these two exhaust the alternatives? This old question again between the universal and the particular, between organism and its various organs! The dilemma is a self-made one, not arising in the nature of the case, but in setting the particular over against the whole.

99. Put in practical terms, sovereignty can neither be identified with ethical ideals nor popular aspiration, nor with government. The general will is the only possible sovereign, as Rousseau said, but it is never a mere general something or ideal, but it is the end in effective operation. This statement is formal but is capable of specification, while Rousseau's general will was not. The government is not only not the sovereign, it is also not the legal sovereign. The government is simply an institution among other institutions.

100. Sovereignty is in the interaction. It manifests itself in various institutions or habits. Conflicts naturally arise between various institutions. Most of the difficulties will be solved on the basis of custom. At such times the government is at a minimum. Such was the condition in the Roman Empire: general reliance on customs.

101. [What if] there are too many customs not adapted to each other and they must conflict? Then we have to have a formal principle for the adaptation: That is, the end of social action is wider physically than it is psychologically. For example, our own country. Great changes have been going on in the last hundred years. We have here a physical unity over the whole country, but there is no psychological end as comprehensive as the physical. Where customs can't be relied on, then some particular institution must make the bridge over from custom to conscious recognition. Then we have extension of the function of government. Government is no more an organ of sovereignty than the family or business corporation; but it is as an organ of the organ[ism] that has as its work the adaptation of one organ to another in their functioning. Consequently, the relative importance of its function depends upon the things to be adapted.

102. The fallacy of socialism consists in identifying this formal adaptation of social habits to each other, with their organic adaptation. It throws the main emphasis on one part, in this case, on the government. The fallacy of anarchy arises in ignoring the necessity of such a formal institution in bringing new ends to consciousness and defining them. What government actually does is, at time of confusion, to facilitate and accelerate the coming to consciousness of the unity which will unite. So socialism says it is the unity and all the rest is confusion; and anarchism says unity can't be put into society but must be there.

103. Sovereignty in terms of social psychology means that the value of an individual does not attach to it as individual but because of its interpretation in the social organism. The value is the interpretation of the individual through his place in the social sphere. The same is true of institutions. The statement that sovereignty is absolute means that the above statement is unqualifiedly true. The whole individual significance is lost in the social whole. If we take Locke, that sovereignty is to keep the individual's position intact, the fallacy is in supposing again that there is a . . .

104. . . . [un]ity[42] in the rhythmical process of development.[43] It differentiates again with necessity of continual reconstruction, or re-adaptation. Now this involves necessarily a falling apart of habits and ideals. Now so far as habit (the already formed, etc.) isn't flexible and resists in consciousness, that is, so far it will present itself as force [contrary] to the ends of reconstruction. The social organism presents itself to any individual as force whenever there is conflict of

habits. In one sense there is nothing but force: in some sense of force as activity. But this activity or force will present itself as force in the sense of coercion whenever there is a conflict. Force, then, is never a bare physical fact but always the felt tension: the tension in consciousness between habit and ideals. What will appear as force depends upon our standpoint. If we identify ourselves with the reformers and progressives, the persistence of the old institutions will appear as force. If we identify ourselves with [the] habit side, [we] are conservative, and the new attempts will appear as force.[44]

105. When the process of reconstruction goes on, some individual is individualized, and it gets an initiative in action which it has not had before. Say this individual is an institution. It becomes the center for experimenting along new elements. Given an individual who is thus varying, and it is bound to run against the fixed side. There must not only be initiation, but there must be reflection which gives the direction. The extent to which the experiment will be of value is in so far as he can translate that opposition into his own means for his activity.

106. The initiative is at first blind. The reflection makes it possible to make the objective clear and defined, and then be made a basis for further action. In so far as the individual can use the opposition for his stimuli to utilization, the social forces will present themselves as subservient to his own interests. And so [with] history. When Hobbes laid down sovereignty as force, Locke soon after says it is subservient means to the individual. In history, these two usually balance each other. They both have the same assumption at bottom. That is the externality of the individual and society. One fixed at one stage, the other at another. That is all the difference. We have in Rousseau still another view. Here we have the dawning consciousness of a common end amid the diversity of classes. The general will was identified with the end, and so everything else was uncalled for. Here he shows his double position: on the one hand the attacker on all existing means and on the other the prophet of a brotherhood. So socialism and anarchism both took their rise in Rousseau.

[Chapter 12. The Moral and the Legal as Phases in the Reconstruction of the Ethical]

107. We saw that in the consideration of the reconstruction of society, when readjustments are at their height, it differentiates into habits and ideas.[45] This gives the basis for the distinction between the *de facto* and *de jure*. The ideal which emerges in the conflict constitutes the *de jure* phase; and that which furnishes the means for realizing the ideal is the *de facto* phase. The whole process may be termed ethical. The legal and the moral are phases of the reconstruction of the ethical. The moral signifies the conscious side, while the ethical signifies the whole institutional adjustment. We are not conscious of the process; we grasp the outcome only, consciously. When the conflict comes in, then the method becomes conscious. This reflection on activity, bringing out the technique, is the legal phase. It is a mode of existing activity. The legal is the condition for further action. It is what the individual may count upon in realizing his end. It enables him to place himself. The positive value of legality is in putting at disposal of the individual the technique which society has worked out.

108. In this interpretation of the legal, the illegitimate use of it consists in transforming this functional fixity of existence. That is, the legal gives the end, instead of really defining the means so as to help the individual to work out his own ends. The moral in its legitimate sense is the realization of the end which will satisfy the conditions, that is, [that] which will freely function the conditions of action. In this sense there is the interaction between the means and ends. Society has certain ends and then takes a survey of what is on hand to realize it.

109. To take up again legal fallacy: It consists in supposing that we have some criterion for determining the legal apart from the ends which society has. It is the historical fallacy again.[46] We insert into the process the outcome of the process. From the psychological standpoint, the legal corresponds to the scientific standpoint, that is, which determines the conditions of action. When the legal is thus solidified on the one side, the moral is sure to get thrown out of joint on the other. The moral is not interpreted as perception of the movement, but as simply the desirable, that is, the abstract, remote, purely objective ideal.

110. Here we get a rank radical as opposed to a rank conservative. The moral in reality is always simply [the] solution of the situation. It never exists in [the] abstract. It is always, like the legal, relative. The formulation of the ideal consists in bringing movement enough to consciousness to handle present conditions.

You can't formulate the ideal as ideal. We try to get out of this particular period of time and get hold of [the] social process in general form. Then we have so much technique. The legal process is never a process of simply re-assertion of what is already law. The application which the judge makes is never simply mechanical, but always organic. It always means a making over of the working hypothesis.

111. So the moral process is never the mere assertion of the ideal as such, but is the use of the ideal to manipulate the conditions. The legal or judicial movement is deductive or synthetic. Moral movement is inductive or analytic. The legislative process is in a certain sense the moral process.

112. Historically, there have been four main types regarding legal and moral:

1. The theory just stated, which makes function between the two being social action. Plato, Aristotle.
2. The theory which asserts a complete duality between moral and legal. The moral is purely subjective means of conscience, and the legal is so much external existence. This is complete dualism.
3. The type represented by the Greek sophists, and then Hobbes, that the legal absolutely determines the moral. Whatever that State commands is the right, and vice versa. The above[47] set up individual conscience, and the third is the reaction against that. That is what Hobbes did, and set [a] limit to individual variation in the government.
4. The theory of Kant and T. H. Green which attempts to separate and yet relate the two. Moral lies in motive and is individual in nature. But say we also have to take into account the realization of that motive; and so legal, while not moral, it must give a minimum of obstruction to the ethical ideal. According to Green, the moral relates to the motive and disposition which is formed in the individual, and the legal and political is outside the moral sphere in one sense; but since it is to be the instrument for the realization of the moral good, it has a moral criterion. (Section V, p. 39, *Lectures on Political Obligation*).[48] The legal and political cannot be in the moral sphere. The law can only regulate outward acts, and they only are grounds of legal obligation. Green continually oscillates between the two. Page 36 and 37 treats of the legal as only external, while the moral takes hold of the internal. In the first place, external and internal are terms which have meaning only functionally, not fixed.

113. Sections 11, 12, 13. At the end of Section 12 he carries legal action clear over into consciousness. He finally says that law has to do with intention, but not with motive.

114. We have seen that motive is intention.[49] You can't make a moral distinction between what a man intends and why he intends (motive). This distinction reduces itself to a change from an abstract to a completer view of the act. On the

practical side, Green says law does not care for motive but that the act be performed. But the only guarantee that the acts will be performed is the motives.
The law stopping with intention, as distinct from motive, doesn't deal with the
real intention.

115. Morality, no more than legality, has anything to do with any thing[s?]
other than the performance of acts. Whichever is taken, acts and motives cannot be separated. The actual distinction between legal and moral is a practical
one. The judge and jury go as far into motives and inner workings of criminals
as the knowledge of psychology will allow.

116. The history of judicial proceedings shows that the standard of judgment
has changed continually. [The history of the relation of] law and equity is a good
illustration. Law is the psychology of several centuries back. In order to use the
[new] psychology, of the equity, [actual equity?] is put as not legal. But after
awhile, what was equity becomes law, and this is but a continual narrowing of
the distance between legal and moral. The moral is complete insight into the act
of man. The legal is not. It is the formulation of the insight of the previous period. Appendix I of Green shows this oscillation between moral and legal.[50]

117. This brings us again to relation of force and idea. What is the moral significance of force? What does it mean in social development? It is the demand
made on the attention of the individual when it is following its habitual line.

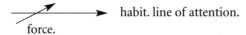 habit. line of attention.

force.

The social criterion of force is the extent to which it is able to suggest ends
for attention. Where society comes down as mere force in the individual, it is
defective; that is, unable to so organize force as to give the most economical
system of demands on attention of the individual. Vid.[51] Education is better
than punishment because it is more economical. The family involves exactly
the same use of force as the state. Green calls family moral but state legal. In
other words, force as mere force is no more legal than moral. It represents mere
loss of energy.

118. The economic aspect of society is the distribution and arrangement of
force. If these are true, the effective regulation of society tends to pass into the
industrial interaction, that is, in getting a living. Ninety percent of the force
which leads man to go along orderly is found in the industrial discipline. It has
become organized into the social structure itself. The political system may be
regarded as the social structure considered as an instrument for maintaining the
ends that are regarded as worthwhile. The legal is the institution considered as
formulated. The moral is the determination of the end for which the legal may
be made.

119. At the saturation stage, there is no felt or recognized distinction between means and ends. After we transcend this state we can look back on it and analyze out the means and ends. In the elaborative or indicative stage, a distinction arises between ideas on one side and force on the other.[52] In other words, will, in certain phases of its development, means nothing but free expression of force.

120. The other phase of the development of will is when it takes the form of effort on one side and desire on the other. When it takes this latter form, the distinction between the force aspect and idea aspect arises. Here is also the basis for the distinction of T. H. Green's inner and outer. Hence the falsity of Kant and Green of the force of "external" as necessary to carry out the impulse and disposition and yet [which] does not enter into the formation of it.

121. The end or aim set up, consciousness, always represents some attained value. Instead of being internal as against external, it is a certain situation realized. That is, the internal now is a combination of the internal and external of previous situations. This means that the motive which a class has, at a given time, is the expression of habits. Supposing that such a motive meets resistance, what happens? In case of meeting resistance, the individual attempts to so redefine his motives as to include these resistances within them. The individual stops to think. An absolutely unmodified motive would be analogous to the condition of man's maniac or hypnotized person. Whether we take original outgrowth of motive or content, it always takes up into itself the conditions: that which Green and Kant rule out as external.

122. The idea, instead of being something set over against the force side, is the force side arranged. It is a plan of how to coordinate the forces. The thought side is the plan. In the saturation stage, the person's ruling ideas represent the forces of habit. The elaboration stage is a coordination of all. Any other doctrine leads to the fallacy of good intentions. In this process of transformation, the tension will be located in accordance with interest. That is, the interest in one class may be predominately in the assertion of one of the already realized values; hence the realized end (being the outcome of the previous situation) will run up against the existing mechanism. That means there are no crimes now which were not virtues at some previous period. Crime means a return to a previous order of society unmediated with present conditions. At the opposite pole from the criminal is the conscientious conservative, that is, the man who consciously asserts values which have been worked out by society because deemed necessary to the maintenance of society. See Burke's attitude to the French Revolution. Here it is not against, but for the sake of, social structure.

123. The reflective abstraction of movement gives rise to three types. As against the criminal type we have the moral reformer or hero, who asserts the ideal movement so that he carries into conflict with the mechanism of the ex-

isting structure; so that it turns upon him just as it does upon the criminal. This is exertion in one direction. In contrast to that we have the wrongdoing of good people, that is, the deadness of good ideals, and getting emotional values in it without using it as a guide to action. Against the conservative we have the liberal who believes in more or less change.

[Chapter 13. Classifications of Rights and Duties]

124. A system of rights and duties is the organization by which members of the social organism reciprocally stimulate and control each other's actions. It is impossible in this to separate the idea and the mechanism side. One individual can't stimulate another directly.[53] There must be some medium of interaction. Things and objects are those media. The object represents simply the meeting point or means of adjustment between individuals. The question, then, of the system of law, the positive structure in which society is organized, involves the consideration of the relationship between the individual and the thing or object. There is always no direct relation between the individual and the thing. [The] thing is the basis for the relation between different individuals. It is recognized as the thing because it stands for the tension.

125. *[1. Rights of persons and rights of things]* [First,] shall [we] use, then, as a basis for classification of rights and duties, this distinction between individual and thing? (See also Holland's *Jurisprudence.*)[54] The rights of person means status. The rights of things means sphere for exercise of activity. Status is a definite system of objects, control over which is assured to the individual by society. See also the different status of child and adult. The rights of things simply means the status in operation. That is, instead of facts which society puts at his disposal, it is his disposal of these things. The fallacy which arises here is the separation of the two. The further question is: Why has the basis of classification lost caste? It is not that status is no longer important, but it is because the status has changed from physical to organic. In older forms, status was predetermined by conditions which we could now call physical: birth, blood, etc.

126. *[2. Rights in rem and in personam]* Now the quality of status has changed. In mobile society, the individual, in working out his experience, finds what objects he can control, and so through himself determines his status. In the distinction, as a working legal basis, there are very few things which can be pre-determined, and so that basis has tended to disappear. The basis of class now is right *in rem* and *in personam*. The first is right which holds one thing as against every other claim. The second holds good only against some special person's rights. Family [rights] are rights *in personam*. The first are general, the second specific. The first can be stated only in negative terms, the second in positive. As regards philosophical significance of these classes the rights *in rem* represent the formed habits, that is, we can count on them for the most part without con-

sideration. The right *in personam* is the right which relates to future rather than that fixed by past, which involves the development to some end. That is, it is bringing the rights *in rem* to a head. Because of the correlativity between the two, there is constant interaction. The real problem of social organization is to keep these [the correlativity between the two?] in both.[55]

127. *[3. Antecedent and remedial rights]* The third point of view from which rights have been classified are as antecedent and remedial. As technically used, antecedent is right as such and remedial is the right to have the right enforced. [An] axiom of law is: "Right which has not its mode of execution defined is not a right." In regard to this distinction, in every progressive society conflict of rights must arise. In stationary society there need be no conflict theoretically. But in progressive society, exercise of right extends the situations. Then between these two situations there is a sphere where individuals may come into conflict. It is a phase of tension in growth. The legislative function is the attempt to define conditions of exercise of rights for the minimum conflict. But in progressive society it must always be either behind or ahead. Hence judicial function comes in, which is day-by-day re-definition of right.

128. The legislative and judicial functions represent the two phases: the first to avoid conflict by anticipation, and the latter to reconstruct where conflict occurs. The decision of the conflict defines the rights. The conflict arises because of the very indefiniteness of the right. It is not simply in the interest of the individual that the remedial right has place, but equally in interest of society as a whole, because of two reasons: (1) Because the individual is an organ in society, and any hurt to him is hurt to society; (2) It is to the interest of society to have the rights of individuals defined. It is perhaps more important to society as a whole than to any individual to have rights defined. Social action based on vague rights is uncertain.

129. Distinction between crimes and torts. The legal distinction is that crimes have remedy in form of punishment: damages given, loss made good. On the psychological side, whatever is regarded as crime is taken as indicating an anti-social motive; it is taken as generalized, as against any others of society. Hence the appeal is by society. Society has been threatened. And so the individual cannot take compensation for the crime or he becomes criminal. In the case of tort, there is no indication of a motive threatening to society as a whole, but against special individuals. Here the burden is thrown on the aggrieved individual. That is, if you don't care enough about it to remedy it, we can stand it. The practical psychology of this is that it makes a further development or responsibility. It is the distinction again between general conditions of action and specific acts.

130. *[4. Personal rights and political or public rights]* The fourth basis of classification is into personal rights or private rights, political rights [or] civil rights. First [are] like life, liberty, the pursuit of happiness. Political or public rights are right[s] of suffrage, that is, the right to participate in some overt way in determination of law. The distinction between them can only be a functional distinction, and not fixed as is usually held. All rights should be both public and private. The distinction is simply the old question of the relation of individual to society. The exercise of private right ought to add to the social consciousness. The political philosophy of the seventeenth and eighteenth century was based on the theory that an individual had an existence apart from society. Natural rights has no significance in itself today. Almost every state constitution has some clause on natural rights based as they are on eighteenth century theory.

131. Political rights (sixteenth century) were theoretically formulated after sovereignty had been established. The whole theory of the French Revolution was: There are such and such natural rights, and therefore political rights should be so and so. The so-called private rights represent the focus, and the political rights the ultimate conditions from that. In order for man to have his private rights, he must keep control of the conditions of action and so must participate in political rights.

132. To summarize. There are two points of view for considering these distinctions. From one point, the two are phases: the personal being the phase where the individual gets return to himself of content of his acting, while the public right represents his value in determining society. The individual is following his own sphere of action in determining society. From the other point of view, they represent two stages in the development of action, and not two phases: development of right representing in this case the summed up right in this organization, and the political right or law representing the sphere of action which the individual must get in relation to, in order to insure his private rights. The four principles are lines according to which rights have been considered historically.

133. *[5. Nominal rights and actual rights]* There is another distinction between nominal rights and actual rights. Nominal rights are those in which the individual is theoretically free to act. It is negative as far as there is no working guarantee that he can use it. The actual rights do not have this negative aspect. If the man has to live in bad conditions, his life is only nominal.

134. [You] can't classify rights in hierarchical series. Every right implies all others. It is fallacious that one right can be realized without others. A particular right is where sovereignty is focusing at [a] particular time.

135. Is a re-adjustment of rights necessary, and how it is best brought about? These are two questions which arise in any question of change, like governmental control of railroads. The nominal right is an expression of the extent of conflict between classes in the social organism, expressing the dependence of any one right on all others. Conflict of classes will come in because some other possesses as actual right what this individual possesses only as nominal right.

[Chapter 14. Rights in Particular]

136. If we attempt to classify rights in particular, we see that rights are organs through which social will is maintained and expresses itself. In every stage of reconstruction, this will appear on one side as ideal and on the other as force. [We] have the following types.

1. Rights to life, that is, control of body.
2. Rights to property.
3. Rights to free locomotion.
4. Rights to contract.
5. Rights to status.
6. Rights of permanent association.
7. Right to calling.
8. Right of expression.
9. Political rights.[56]

This classification is made on the basis of going from the particular side of an act to universal conditions which give it its validity and value.

137. *[1. The right to life]* Take first the fundamental right. In one sense this right is secured, however, only as one has the others. Give the individual a right to life and you create a demand for the right to property, to free locomotion, etc.[57] Each right is taken as means to further end. The right to life represents the fundamental means to be utilized.

138. *[2. Rights to property]* Property right is the extension of the same right to life. Property right represents the basic objectification of will. The essence of property is the projection of self into nature. The standard of property right always comes back to the question of how much control the individual needs to realize himself. Only then have you a limit to property right. The private side of property right is the side of initiative and possession. The public side is side of use and exercise. Hence the fallacy of an employer in a strike to say it is his own business.

139. Take the ownership side in relation to communism. If you don't secure to the individual a certain amount as his own, how is society going to get a purchase on him? Property is the way through which society can touch a person and get his attention to something. If you eliminate that, as in communism, there is no room for society to stimulate the thoughts of an individual in certain directions. All communistic schemes always assume their character as de-

veloped on the basis of property and then cut loose [the individual?]. Only through natural forces do ideas become effective so that people get the value of them more than individual feeling at the moment. This is an important part of social mechanism. Anything that stimulates the individual to greater utilization of natural force is of greatest importance.

140. Continuing discussion of personal property, it, as represented in growing coordination of natural forces being affected through ideas, may have another classification according to the stage arrived at of synthesis between physical and ideal element.

141. *[a. Land]* The most physical and immediate phase [or type] is that which relates to land. Because this is the most direct contact between two sides, organism and environment, it is an instrument of higher mediation of mere ideal elements. It is the condition of all further coordination. Therefore the question of property is most acute. The whole question of the evolution of property rights is bound up with the question of individual's ends or aims to control the parts. Shall it be attained directly or indirectly? Can the land question be solved by itself once for all? Or can it be attained only indirectly through the reaction of further evolution of wealth into this world? In economics, it is a question of relation between product, distribution, and consumption. Are they so many independent processes or stages in development? It would be found historically that the adjustments that have come on the side of land have been through the reaction of industries back on it, giving new value. It is impossible to study the landed question by itself and represent [this] phase in the realization of Values.

142. *[b. Manufacture and distribution]* The second type in this process of coordination is [the] mediating phases: manufacture and distribution agencies which take the above wealth of products and place them further in their coordination, that is, extending it over larger area. Evolution of capital at this point is significant. Capital represents the elimination of time, just as machinery represents elimination of space. Capital is the ability to discount time ahead and make it cover a definite space of time. Aside from this in some form, there is no time coordination.

143. Machinery is unification of the environmental side constituting a larger environment. This type may be called mediating type because it represents a balance between ideal and physical side. In agriculture, in first stage the physical predominates over the ideal. Here, area is comparatively small, agricultural community necessarily limited. It is only through the commercial setting up of relations between these segregated communities that environment is enlarged. Where[58] . . . . . . pendant on habit. Let area be extended, the economic

struggle becomes one to make a market and not an habitual adjunct to existing market. It is necessarily parallel with a scientific development. There is no inherent reason why a man in 1800 A.D. wants to get [control over more?] whole earth than in 1800 B.C. [We] have to bring in scientific development to explain it. Force gets its impedance through the extension of science.

144. *[c. Ideas separated from action]* In the third type, we may say ideas predominate and don't get balanced: embodiment instead of being executive. An idea appears in terms of itself instead of in terms of action. That is practically the state of things today. There is little commercial value attached to the idea; that is, the thinker is supported on a subsidized plan, instead of being in commercial demand. This shows that yet there is separation between theory and practice. Otherwise the commercial demand for truth would keep the truth factory going as well as common demand for ploughs keeps the plower factory going. The analysis relates more to present conditions of things.

145. The over-physical side of the first type is offset by the ideal side of the third type, and so the intermediate class gets the benefit of both. It exploits both the agricultural class on one side and the thinking class on other; that exploitation showing that here balance between the two has been most successfully kept. This is banking, railroad, and manufacturing type. It hasn't been the scientific man that got rich, nor even the inventor.

146. The over-materialistic phase of commerce is simply balance of over-abstract phase of ideas. The scientific formula is obviously abstract because it is general. The class which takes the idea and applies it is doing more concrete thinking. Because the thinker is subsidized he does not come in contact with concrete facts. If he does, he becomes a moral reformer. He doesn't run the risk of experimentation of the commercial man. The embodiment of idea means that the individual is thinking in social terms instead of merely physical terms. It is one thing to make an invention. It is another to introduce it. The present state of things with the property question is not anything absolute but is relative fact ultimately dependent on the development of science. The development of physical science has outrun the development of social science, that is, the earth has become one physically but has not become one intellectually.

147. The price of wheat in Chicago is changed by conditions in China. In other words, it has become a world market. The organization of intelligence has lagged behind the extension of physical environment; so the tension between the two. The concrete social science would mean the actual organization of society. We have now only the method of social science. It is evident that in such a period the element of risk is at the maximum. What the period at present means is that the environment has extended over the whole earth and so the

tensional element is there. But the functional element is not and can't be until the whole is organized so that the individual knows where he is in the system. That is, you have to know time conditions as well as space conditions. He has to know where he is now. This is the province of newspapers.

148. Locomotive and telegraph have made it [the world] physically one, and are means whereby it can be made intellectually one by distribution of mails, etc. But at present it is very inchoate. So far as the newspaper attempts to influence opinion instead of simply giving news, it is not on [a genuine] commercial basis. Its only commodity ought to be truth.

149. Spencer, Chapters 6, 7, 8, 9, of *Principles of Sociology*, Vol. I.[59] Given: (1) sustaining, (2) distributing, (3) regulating systems. The principle of development in the first system is adaptation. In the second, the blood system in the animal organism, highways, steamboats, etc. Then the banking system is parallel to vaso-motor system. The sustaining system corresponds to the outer layer in the animal organism, and the inner has two types in the social organism. This, like similar subdivision in political economy, represents phases and not separate processes. The sustaining system has no ultimate value in itself. It is because they can distribute better. That is, the one system represents the other side of the other system. Since these stages are references to a common end, the attainment of a higher life value, the sustaining and distributing systems can do really[60] their parts, but [only] in so far as there is a social sensorium. This Spencer denies.

150. If you have any division of labor you have to have some principle of division, that is, the activity of each one in the community has got to be controlled by demands made by the community as a whole and by the demands of others. This means that there must be a social sensorium. Spencer says that the process of adjustment is competitive (p. 502). Each organ appropriates a certain amount of the common goods. This is true of animal organisms. Now it is evident that you can't have natural order unless there is some sort of equilibrium maintained; can't have relative starvation at one point without overloading at another.

151. [The] question is how is the relation between supply and demand to be maintained? Spencer assumes that competition will do it. The reason the lungs, heart, etc., don't get all [i.e., everything] for themselves respectively is because there is the nervous system which acts as umpire. That is the reason there is a working equilibrium established. Why doesn't a man make too many plows, or too few, for the community? Because of the social sensorium, that is, the individual controls his manufacture by feeling the demand of the community. When you get the first physical extension, it outruns the development of sen-

sorium and the competition becomes more or less pathological. The so-called identity of the individual and social interests of the Manchester school would not be true except on basis of social sensorium: [the] basis on which individual can't know his interests except through social interests.

152. In the same way, to make a purely socialistic scheme to work [there] must be a basis of social consciousness. What is the means of getting this social intelligence? Would it be a special organ as so-called socialistic government? Or will it be simply in the interaction of parts? The last is true. The socialistic fallacy in logic is the confusions of ends with means. The end must be social so they interpret the means also as social. At a certain stage of development the social intelligence may not become distributed and an individual having this fore-knowledge and acting upon it may become rich. Cf. Rothchilds. The point is that the controlling power in the distribution of industrial system will always be the existing social sensorium.

153. Regarding the direction of government function, it is obvious that government function tends to increase in such a period; its function being to limit this fluctuation. But will not government function direct itself most widely in such periods in the direction of publicity, that is, make things known? Cf. census reports. In other words, Spencer's third system (regulating system)[61] can only be the social sensorium.

154. To sum up the matter of property: The distinction between nominal property and the actual or working property right is important. The latter is a function of the whole social organization, and simply defines the way in which the attained adjustment of individual and environment has acted on the individual to give it new value. The attempt to abstract the property question by itself as so much attained material which is to be distributed among a certain number is impossible. It is material because it isolates a certain form of social value as an entity. Primary socialism must be a socialism of intelligence, that is, it must place at the disposal of the individual knowledge of the whole. The logic of extreme individualism and extreme socialism are one; only one lauds it and the other condemns it.

155. Question of labor: From an objective point of view labor is one form of physical energy, as steam, etc. The fact that the energy expresses itself through natural body does not change its form. It is fully as important that energy should be free and properly coordinated as the energy in steam, etc., should be.

156. Division of labor is simply the freeing and coordinating of this energy. The next point is that division of labor regarded as economic is not complete till it is completely individualized. That is, we don't get the most of energy till it is changed from motor to molecular, and that means that the individual acts

with least resistance. As it does this, the energy passes from muscular to nervous system. In the muscular it is still in gross form. So long as the division of
labor is on the muscular side, that is, simply doing what others are not, the ability to think and initiate is left out of account. The principle of division of labor,
once entered upon, must mean the completest freeing of the individual possible.

157. Can't get the best out of anybody while he is under external control.
Thus, while labor work does represent a form of physical energy, yet in the fact
that this particular form of energy is its embodiment in nervous system, it gets
a greater predominance in efficiency, although it is on par in principle with other
forms of energy. It is that on which the efficiency of the other forms depend.

158. The individual must be set more and more free to make a minimum
amount of friction and waste of energy. The ideal of proper development is in
the first place that the individual should have sufficient tools and media to express himself in the most immediate way, and one point of the tools is control
of his own brain and muscles; and, second, that he shall have reflected back to
him the social value of what he is doing. If any individual can thus work at his
full capacity and gets social recognition of its value, the question of wealth has
no meaning. If he has what he wants, he does not care how much there is that
he does not want.

159. This is continuance of evolution. The bearing of the above on the question of value is an important question. Value here is what it is everywhere: realization in consciousness. Political economy would seem [to be] the means of
comprehending this value. Immediate values all stand on the same level. As social consciousness develops, it becomes less immediate. That is, it has a larger
range of choice. The whole reign of exchange value is unfolding and enlarging
of ultimate values; or it represents, controls the ability to determine future value
and to get greater meaning out of the present by seeing its relation to past and
future. The act of measure reacts into and enlarges the values themselves.

160. If man did not have to work for a living and could satisfy appetites as they
arise, the wants would all be on the same level, and it would never enter anyone's head to find which want was most important. When we have to labor to
satisfy them, the last comes in. The fundamental economic fallacy is the assumption that [the] sense of value is already there, and that the economic
process only satisfies these [values]. [Rather,] it [the economic process] creates
and develops the sense of value itself. Therefore, ultimately the economic
process is a psychological and ethical one.

161. Property rights have been divided into (1) rights to hold, which is not
complete right; a tenant has a right to hold, (2) right to use, (3) right to alienate, which means to completely determine my relationship to others. This is the

culmination of right. In other cases, another will can enter into to limit. Just as the right to property is necessary to the right to free activity, so [we] can't have complete property right without having rights to locomotion and rights to contract—which will be discussed later.

162. What is the psychological value of the wealth doctrine of property, that is, the tension relation between increase of property and means of support? What is the meaning that you have to hypotenate[62] capital to labor, that is, one presupposes the other?

163. *[3. The rights to locomotion]* Rights of free locomotion, contract. First, is outgrowth, and the necessity for the two classes of rights previously spoken of. It is nothing but the explicit statement of right to have will at all. The main interest, therefore, attaches to the historical development of the right, and the various forms in which it has been made concrete in different periods. This is the history of the environment, of the social organism, from local land with which they had direct contact to the comparatively world-wide environment. There is of course the question of how far there are instruments for free locomotion. In this historical development the right to free locomotion means the ability to select environment. It means that of necessity there is a tremendous development of the individual. All great intellectual and political outbursts have come because the means of locomotion had been greatly extended. Conflict between different ideas and habits means a tremendous shaking up of both. Cf. Renaissance. The religious, ethical, and moral truths, etc., modify each other.

164. Free locomotion is life in its external side. Right of contract is the right to control certain natural objects in reference to another will. Mere appropriation never constitutes property. It has also to be recognized. The right to property, more specifically, finds its expression in the right to alienate. Every buying and selling implies the contract relation.

165. *[4. Rights to contract]* The significance of contract right is that it brings to overt recognition all the rights implicit in all property rights. Property is projection of one's purposes into natural forces. Contract is the mediation of the controls of two or more individuals. It is an exchange of services under specified conditions. Contract rights (determination of social relations) will come to focus only when the individual has become [a] specialized center of control. In the sixteenth and seventeenth centuries when the contract theory of the state was formulated, this exact condition existed. The individual was emerging to its objective status. So from the time of Hobbes to 1800, somewhat over 200 years, the contract doctrine was the doctrine. The individuals were centers of control. Then mind had to image some relation between one another. Contract theory is based on just this, in working relations between centralized individuals. But

that contract arises out of instinctive association and has its value in bringing to recognition the instinctive association.

166. The fallacy of contract theory is that they suppose society to grow out of society, while contract presupposes the association is instinctive. The social habit and individual aim become more and more consciously the same. The commercial exchange development, and development of contract, parallel and necessitate each other.

167. The nature of contract, while extending the special area of the individual, is to steady time relation. The socialistic state would have to substitute something to take the place of contract to keep time relation stable and enable a man to direct his activity today with reference to something in the future. The whole tendency is to neglect the psychological factors involved, that is, consider it as mere mechanism. The constant stimuli to attention must be taken into account in order to keep the mechanism going. The individual's greatest attention is to activity itself and not to the product. Therefore, the manufacturer doesn't work to get the greatest amount of product in money, but has the product as a stimulus to keep up the activity.

[Chapter 15. Competition and Education as Factors in the Selection and Evolution of Social Callings]

168. Proper education may solve many of the difficulties which appear in socialism. For example, how is an individual going to know what he is best fitted for? There must be some mechanism in society by which the individual can judge his own work. The first, the continuity of social habits, is one of the strongest in the past. Enlarge your environment, and the individual has more to select from. He has all kinds of pursuits put before him as possibilities.

169. The second main reliance is education, which tends to replace the above. Then the whole import of education changes. The old theory of education was to equip the individual to carry out a predetermined end. When it becomes means for making new ends, it becomes: How shall we, in an ordered way, bring the individual into contact with the typical activities of a free society so that he may find his own tastes and capacities? This is another important phase of the social sensorium. With such systematic organization of education making continually regulated contact of individual with activities, the range of competition would be tremendously lowered. The individual would start in his purposive [activities][63] with so much knowledge ahead; so experimentation in after-life would be minimized. But the question still remains whether that would fully solve the problem. That is, what would be the stimulus to new callings? Or in other words, bring to consciousness of society new wants? In the past, competition has been the main way of securing variation.

170. Competition and education are the only two methods so far employed to bring the individual to consciousness of social need in order to select a calling. Education brings the child into touch with all occupations. When this is systematized it will do away to a great extent with competition. But it is impossible to do away with competition entirely in the process of evolution of a calling. Education will decide the adaptation of the individual to calling. But a further stimulus is necessary to variation and development of new callings. Education is on the static side, or side which determines the conditions. In the education stage, society places its forces at the disposal of the individual. The individual is not supposed to be productive, that is, society does not expect returns from its expenditure at the time. It is too organic to be called charity, however. The fact that it is the period for the individual to master his own powers, makes the process distinctly a conservative process. That does not detract from the fact that education is one of the most progressive of elements in the process. So far

as society is concerned, education may be a tremendous instrument of progress, but it is not by stimulating the individual to new lines of activity but by transferring his past experience into terms of idea.

171. When it comes to the question of product as such, or the question or varying or multiplying sources at the disposition of society, [there is] another kind of stimulus. In principle, one phase is distinguished from another by the fact that in the education period society takes its standard environment and puts the child in it. And in the other the individual becomes independent center of reflection and initiation for creating new environment. This is the element of competition which is striving together, and not apart, as is popularly thought. A new calling is an industrial invention just as much as a new machine is. It covers periods[64] to new variations of species in the animal world. At present there is no such balance between education and competition. The more established industries ought to tend[65] less and less out of competitive form. But in industries when the best modes of production are fairly well worked out, competition would be only [a] source of disorder. But take industries in which invention is still going on, when it is still [a] problem which is the best method of production, competition [is] about the only thing that can stimulate to development.

172. The retail system is a survival of custom. Clerks in a country store can tell within six spools of thread how much will be bought. A few years ago this was the case all over the country. Now it is not, and we are surviving the form without content.

[Chapter 16. Permanent Associations]

173. The next phase of organization is permanent associations. This [gives?] balance to the contract relationship. The strong point about the last was it gave definite statement of time and amount so that present conditions can be made for future. But it can only cover special acts because of its definiteness.

174. Three typical forms are: family, industrial, church. So far as society becomes free, the family must take its rise from contract in form. But in content the association is too intimate to state in contract. The current orthodox theory of family and state is so-called patriarchal, that is, that family is state in minimum, then clan, then city, and then state developed in order. Sir Henry Maine is the great modern representative of this.

175. According to this, family is a type of political structure. According to others, patriarchal does not represent primitive but a quite advanced stage of development. This has [a] horde theory with promiscuity of sexual relation, with no permanent relation between father and mother to children, but only mother and children (as chickens).

176. Later research does not go to the extreme of either theory. The patriarchal theory has been overthrown as primitive. It is the outcome of considerable social consolidation. Neither is horde theory considered in any way universal. If [sexual relations][66] showed this, it was degeneracy. Family existed from the beginning. However, matriarchate proceeded patriarchate. The line of descent passed through the mother because paternity was uncertain. Mothers were considered heads of families, and ruled the state.

177. The fallacy of considering family as the source of state is due to thinking of family as a fixed unit, and from [this] combination state arose. This is only true in cross-section; not taking the whole development in society, determined the unity of family. Family has had history, not only as determining society but also as an organ determined by society.

Notes

1. For Dewey's reconstruction of this antagonism, see these lectures, §75, §118.
2. For more on the evolution of commodities, see §142–43.
3. That is, external to the economic process.
4. The word 'order' is crossed out in the typescript and 'idea' is written in above.
5. Presumably a reference to the "evolutionary point of view" in §5.
6. See Edward Alsworth Ross, "Social Control," *American Journal of Sociology* 1 (March 1896): 513–35. This article was later included in Ross's book *Social Control* (New York: Macmillan, 1901).
7. Lester F. Ward, "Sociology and Psychology," in *American Journal of Sociology* 1, *Contributions to Social Philosophy* no. 5 (March 1896): 618–32 . The article was included later as part of Wards's *Outlines of Sociology* (New York: Macmillan, 1898).
8. That is, of dualism.
9. For the development of this view in detail, see the "Lectures on the Logic of Ethics" in this volume, §58–73; see also Dewey's *Logic: The Theory of Inquiry*, where the predicate has the instrumental function "to direct further operations of experimental operation," but its meaning must be "operationally checked" by ascertaining whether the operations it directs "actually cohere in a unified way" (*LW*, 12:134).
10. Presumably Dewey means "different phases of the same process."
11. Herbert Spencer, *First Principles*, 2nd American ed. (Boston: Estes and Lauriat, 1867), chap. 19, §149–69. Apropos of Dewey's argument in this chapter, he says "that Spencer's method of taking groups of facts, apparently wholly unlike each other, such as those of the formation of solar systems, on one side, and facts of present social life, on the other, with a view to discovering what he calls 'some common trait,' has, indeed, more value for philosophic method than is generally recognized." See "The Philosophical Work of Herbert Spencer" (1904), *MW*, 3:205 n.
12. The word 'distinction' is unclear in the carbon copy.
13. Possibly "all things."
14. Possibly Dewey said "objects," but there is a sense in which the object is also an "objection" to the previous functioning of the individual.
15. Presumably, Dewey means "form the environment in terms of organism," as when a potter "throws" a pot.
16. Apparently the functional or structural individual is a "rhythmic process," and the habitual individual is the individual as "attained adjustment" or "concentrated universe," and the objective individual is the "variable" factor.
17. Or, if Dewey is to be consistent, the "transitional species" or "missing link" is an unsuccessful outcome of the objective or initiating factor, so it cannot be found. For more on this, see Dewey's 1898 "Lectures on Political Ethics," *LPPE*, p. 291.

18. The carbon copy is unclear, but it is difficult to give any other interpretation to this word.

19. The term 'ethical statics' refers to the established moral order, taken as if it were stopped in time and not evolving. See Samuel Alexander's discussion of statics in Book II of his *Moral Order and Progress* (London: Trübner, 1889), and the discussion of social statics and social dynamics, §39–41 of these lectures.

20. Probably a reference to James Mark Baldwin, *Mental Development in the Child and the Race* (New York: Macmillan, 1895). Dewey criticizes Baldwin's account of imitation in the 1898 "Lectures on Political Ethics," *LPPE*, pp. 313–18.

21. George Grote, *A History of Greece: From the Earliest Period to the Close of the Generation Contemporary with Alexander the Great*, 4th ed., 10 vols. (London: John Murray, 1872); see also Dewey, *The Study of Ethics: A Syllabus* (1894), *EW*, 4:219–370, especially the criticism of the "fixed self," p. 256. Dewey criticizes James Mark Baldwin's theory of imitation in his 1898 "Lectures on Political Ethics," *LPPE*, pp. 313–18, and his 1900 "Lectures on Psychological Ethics," *LE*, pp. 317–19.

22. According to Dewey, [Ernst Heinrich] Weber's law is that "a 'stimulus' does not give rise to a conscious reaction until its power reaches a certain ratio to the level of that which is already in consciousness of the effected adjustment; so the conscious individual represents a certain variant in social custom—coming consciousness, because it departs to a certain extent from the existing plane of social adjustments." See the 1898 "Lectures on Psychological Ethics," *LPPE*, p. 19, and the discussion in Dewey's *Psychology* (1891), 3rd ed., in *EW*, 2:49–51. According to one statement, the criterion for maximizing utility is that "the utility derived from the final or marginal utility of any good taken into the agent's combination (at the cost of foregoing some quantities of others goods) must be the same as the final utility obtained from any other kind of good at the same marginal cost or sacrifice." See David Baybrooke, "Economics and Rational Choice," vol. 2 of *The Encyclopedia of Philosophy* (New York: Macmillan, 1967), p. 455.

23. Property rights are discussed in these lectures, §138–61.

24. The typescript reads "imitators".

25. Possibly Dewey said "clash".

26. In the typescript, the last two letters of 'individually' are stricken out and replaced by "in," so the final clause of the sentence reads "individual *in* one class opposes another."

27. Presumably a reference to these lectures, §45.

28. Presumably where 'subjective' means "as employed by the subject."

29. Approximately two-thirds of a line in the carbon copy is not legible.

30. Herbert Spencer, *The Principles of Sociology*, 2nd ed., 2 vols. (New York: D. Appleton, 1870–72).

31. M. T. Harris is probably William Torrey Harris, founder of the *Journal of Speculative Philosophy*, who accepted Dewey's first philosophical articles and encouraged him to go into philosophy. F. M. Taylor was an anarchist and writer of a pamphlet titled *The Right of the State to Be: An Attempt to Determine the Ultimate Human Prerogative on*

Which Government Rests (Ann Arbor, 1891), located in the University of Michigan Library, Special Collections, Labadie Pamphlets.

32. Probably Dewey is criticizing a characterization of objectivity as external to or outside of the situation. See these lectures, §109, and the thorough discussion of this topic in the 1900 "Lectures on the Logic of Ethics," *LE*, pp. 63-67.

33. Or possibly "assured rights."

34. Probably Dewey means "supreme force" or "coercive force." See these lectures, §85, and the 1898 "Lectures on Political Ethics," *LPPE*, pp. 409–27, particularly p. 424.

35. William MacKintire Salter, *Anarchy or Government, An Inquiry in Fundamental Politics* (New York: T. Y. Crowell, 1895).

36. For more on the historical fallacy, see these lectures, §109. It is also called the philosophic fallacy in Chapter One of the first edition of *Experience and Nature* (1925), *LW*, 1:389, and the psychologist's fallacy in the 1898 "Lectures on Psychological Ethics," *LPPE*, p. 25, and the 1900 "Lectures on the Psychology of Ethics," *LE*, pp. 103–4.

37. Dewey's article on Austin was originally published in *Political Science Quarterly* 9 (March 1894), and reprinted in *EW*, 4:70–90. The reference to Green is presumably to the extensive discussion of rights in his *Lectures on the Principles of Political Obligation*, vol. 2 of *Works*, (London: Longmans, Green, 1886). See also Henry Sumner Maine, *Lectures on the Early History of Institutions* (New York: Henry Holt, 1888).

38. Page 45 of the typescript is missing.

39. The title is either Dewey's own or perhaps an interpretation by the transcriber. A better title for the chapter would be "From the Theory of Sovereignty to Individual Initiation in the Social Process."

40. Apparently the transcriber failed to capture the end of the sentence.

41. Apparently another reference to Dewey's article on Austin. See §87 and note 37.

42. Page 51 of the typescript is apparently missing, but it is possible that, as indicated by the "un" in brackets, the transcriber made an error in numbering the typed copy, and this sentence is continuous with the last sentence of §103. So the fallacy of supposing there is a unity in a sovereign "keeping the individual's position intact" is similar to the fallacy of socialism in identifying the formal need for government in adapting social habits to each other, instead of the organic or practical process of adaptation (§102). Both Locke and the socialist are incorrect because they ignore the need for individual initiation guided by reflection (§105).

43. The rhythmic process is first introduced in §27. See also the important role of rhythm for Dewey's rejection of the egoistic psychology in the 1898 "Lectures on Psychological Ethics," *LPPE*, p. 212.

44. Dewey discusses force and ideas (or ideals) from the social standpoint in §117 of these lectures.

45. See these lectures, §104.

46. See these lectures, §87.

47. Presumably referring to the first two theories.

48. Green, *Principles of Political Obligation*.

49. Probably a reference to Dewey's Winter Quarter 1896 "Lectures on Psychological Ethics," of which this course is a continuation.

50. Perhaps a reference to chapter 1 of Green's *Principles of Political Obligation*, titled "Private Rights, The Right to Life and Property."

51. Probably *"vide"* or see before, possibly referring to §78, 104.

52. The elaborative phase is the second phase of organic life. See these lectures, §62, 122.

53. This startling assertion is worked out in more detail in chapter 3 of Dewey's *Democracy and Education* (1916), in vol. 9 of *MW*, titled "Education as Direction".

54. Thomas Erskine Holland, *The Elements of Jurisprudence* (Oxford: The Clarendon Press, 1880).

55. Dewey appears to mean that a successful social organization will harmonize the past, habitual element with proposals for the future.

56. Dewey goes on to discuss these rights in more detail as indicated by the numbers in brackets in the title headings. Nominally, the discussion of property rights extends to §161, where the right to locomotion is discussed. But much of the discussion is really about economic power. With regard to the remaining rights, Dewey seems to be more concerned about the conditions under which rights arise than their explicit formulation or enumeration. The rights to status are ignored, and there is a discussion of permanent associations beginning at §162.

57. For the interrelation of different rights, see these lectures, §160, 162.

58. Apparently, a line of typescript was not reproduced in the carbon copy.

59. Herbert Spencer, *The Principles of Sociology* (New York: D. Appleton, 1878).

60. Perhaps Dewey said "realize their parts."

61. See these lectures, §149.

62. Possibly Dewey said "hypothecate."

63. The typescript reads "purposiveative." Perhaps Dewey invented this word.

64. Perhaps Dewey said "compares to" not "covers periods to."

65. The word "tend" is a guess at the obscure typescript.

66. The typescript reads "If sections showed . . ."

Works Cited
in Dewey's Lectures

Index

Works Cited in Dewey's Lectures

1895 Logic of Ethics

Bain, Alexander. *The Emotions and the Will.* London: John W. Parker and Son, 1859.

———. *Moral Science: A Compendium of Ethics.* New York: D. Appleton, 1882.

Baldwin, James Mark. "The Origin of Things." *Psychological Review* 2 (November 1895), or "The Origin of Emotional Expression." *Psychological Review* 1 (November 1894): 610–23.

Bosanquet, Bernard. *Logic: Or, the Morphology of Knowledge.* 2 vols. Oxford: The Clarendon Press, 1888.

Bradley, Francis Herbert. *The Principles of Logic.* 2 vols. London: Kegan Paul, Trench, 1883.

Caird, Edward. *The Critical Philosophy of Immanuel Kant.* 2 vols. Glasgow: James Maclehose and Sons, 1889.

———. "Metaphysics," *Encyclopaedia Britannica.* 9th ed.

Dewey, John. "The Chaos in Moral Training" (1894). Vol.4 of *EW*, 106–118.

———. "Green's Theory of the Moral Motive" (1892). Vol.3 of *EW*, 155–73.

———. "Moral Theory and Practice" (1891). Vol. 3 of *EW*, 93–109.

———. *Outlines of a Critical Theory of Ethics* (1891). Vol. 3 of *EW*.

———. "Self-Realization as the Moral Ideal" (1893). Vol. 4 of *EW*, 42–53.

———. *The Study of Ethics: A Syllabus* (1894). Vol. 4 of *EW*.

Green, Thomas Hill. *Prolegomena to Ethics.* 2nd ed. Oxford: The Clarendon Press, 1884.

Høffding, Harald. "The Principle of Welfare." *The Monist* 1 (July 1891): 525–51.

Holmes, Oliver Wendell, Jr. *The Common Law.* Boston: Little, Brown, 1881.

Kant, Immanuel. *Immanuel Kant's Critique of Pure Reason.* Translated by F. Max Muller. London: Macmillan, 1881.

Lotze, Hermann. *Logic.* Translated by Bernard Bosanquet. 2nd ed. 2 vols. Oxford: The Clarendon Press, 1888.

Mackenzie, John Stuart. *An Introduction to Social Philosophy.* 2nd ed. Glasgow: James Maclehose and Sons, 1895.

———. *A Manual of Ethics.* 2nd ed. London: University Correspondence College Press, 1894.

Martineau, James. *Types of Ethical Theory.* 3rd ed. Oxford: The Clarendon Press, 1889.

Mill, John Stuart. *A System of Logic, Ratiocinative and Inductive: Being a Connected View of the Principles of Evidence and the Methods of Scientific Investigation.* People's Edition. London: Longmans, Green, 1889.

Murray, John Clark. *An Introduction to Ethics.* Boston: De Wolfe Fiske, 1891.

Royce, Josiah. *The Religious Aspect of Philosophy.* Boston: Houghton, Mifflin, 1885.

———. *The Spirit of Modern Philosophy.* Boston: Houghton, Mifflin, 1892.

Ryland, Frederick. *Logic: An Introductory Model for the Use of the University Student.* London: Bell, 1896.

Spencer, Herbert. *The Data of Ethics.* 2nd ed. New York: D. Appleton, 1880.

———. *First Principles.* New York: D. Appleton, 1888.

Venn, John. *The Principles of Empirical or Inductive Logic.* London: Macmillan, 1889.

1896 Political Ethics

Austin, John. *Lectures on Jurisprudence; or, the Philosophy of Positive Law.* 2 vols. London: John Murray, 1869.

Baldwin, James Mark. *Mental Development in the Child and the Race.* New York: Macmillan, 1895.

Dewey, John. "Austin's Theory of Sovereignty." Vol. 4 of *EW*, 70–90.

———. *The Study of Ethics: A Syllabus.* Vol. 4 of *EW*, 219–370.

Green, Thomas Hill. *Lectures on the Principles of Political Obligation,* Vol. 2 of *Works.* London: Longmans, Green, 1886.

Grote, George. *A History of Greece: From the Earliest Period to the Close of the Generation Contemporary with Alexander the Great.* 4th ed. 10 vols. London: John Murray, 1872.

Holland, Thomas Erskine. *The Elements of Jurisprudence.* Oxford: The Clarendon Press, 1880.

Maine, Henry Sumner. *Lectures on the Early History of Institutions.* New York: Henry Holt, 1888.

Ross, Edward Alsworth. "Social Control." *American Journal of Sociology* 1 (March 1896): 513–35.

Salter, William MacKintyre. *Anarchy or Government, An Inquiry in Fundamental Politics.* New York: T. Y. Crowell, 1895.

Spencer, Herbert. *First Principles.* New York: D. Appleton, 1888.

———. *The Principles of Sociology.* 2nd ed. 2 vols. New York: D. Appleton, 1892–93.

Taylor, F. M. *The Right of the State to Be: An Attempt to Determine the Ultimate Human Prerogative on Which Government Rests.* Ann Arbor, Michigan: N.P., 1891.

Ward, Lester F. "Sociology and Psychology." in *American Journal of Sociology* 1, *Contributions to Social Philosophy* no.5 (March 1896): 618–32.

Index

All references to the body of the lectures are by the paragraph number.
References to the editor's introductions are indicated by page (p. or pp.) number.

Lectures on the Logic of Ethics

Lectures on Political Ethics

Donald F. Koch is a professor of philosophy at Michigan State University.
He has edited John Dewey's *Lectures on Psychological and Political Ethics: 1898*
and *Lectures on Ethics: 1900–1901* and is the coeditor, with Warren G. Samuels,
of *Lectures by John Dewey: Moral and Political Philosophy, 1915–1916.*